Ramblings of a boss dog

John Richard Fielding Terry

To Maie
With love from Scotta

31 Augst 2013

Pubished by:
Argent Vulpes Ltd, 6, Westgate, Scotton, Gainsborough, Lincolnshire, DN21 3QX

with assistance from:
Words and Spaces Ltd, 33 Rothbury Road, Scunthorpe, North Lincolnshire, DN17 1EY

Set in Minion Pro 10/14

ISBN: 9781849143912

Cover design by Stuart Pearcey, Words and Spaces Ltd, 01724 352156

Dedication

Ramblings of a boss dog is dedicated to all the dogs that have entered and left my life as I have aged. From Sam the black Labrador thief who could snaffle a whole Scotch pie in his mouth without drooling, through Spot, Stupid and Bitch in Sharjah who used to plan ambushes in the desert sands, to little Ben our first rescue dog who taught us so much to the hundreds of Dalmatians that passed through our lives and the wonderful people who helped us in running a Welfare Charity, this book is dedicated to all of you.

To my wonderful mother who not only had nine children of her own, but who looked after more than fifty unwanted babies and sent them on their way, and to my long-suffering, but gorgeous, wife Joan for putting up with all my trials, travels and tribulations and for giving me my two adorable daughters, Claire Louise and Gemma Kate, and to Claire and Andrew for adding Charlotte to the family and Gemma and Mikey for adding Jack, this book is dedicated to you all.

It is also dedicated to all those I have followed into battle and to those who have wittingly or not, followed me into battle.

Finally it is also dedicated to my friend Stuart Pearcey without whom this book would not look as great as it does. Enjoy the read.

John Terry
Scotton, Lincolnshire
June 2013

Contents

Chapter 1: At the beginning

As anyone who has attended a Toastmasters International course or meeting will tell you, every story or presentation has to have a beginning, middle and an end or climax. So this is my story up to date, and the beginning, I guess, began when my mother, Juliette Lumsden Terry (nee Ewen), whose birthday was the 17th March, met up with an Inland Revenue clerk called Harry Fielding whose birthday was the 22nd March, somewhere in Edinburgh. 283 days later I was the result of that meeting. My mother was a war widow, having lost her husband Kenneth Sidney Terry on the 17th August 1944 when he was killed in an explosion in Normandy, France. My mother was heavily pregnant at that time with my half-sister Sidnie, and also had two other daughters, Gillian and Annette, and was living in Edinburgh having moved from London to escape the V1 Doodlebugs which she described as being terrifying. My Grandfather and Grandmother were also living in Edinburgh but more of them later.

The 21st December 1947 was an awful night in Edinburgh, with heavy snow making travel impossible, so I entered this world in the main bedroom at 1 East Broughton Place, where the family lived, at 01:38 on the 22nd, and thus was born a Capricorn – but only just, being born very close to the cusp.

There are a few stories about my childhood, and living in a house with four females was definitely a challenge, I am told that on one occasion, having been sent out of the house to walk me in my pram, my three sisters returned in triumph without me, but with a moth-eaten old teddy bear that they had swapped me for. My mother's desperate search for me went on for a couple of hours before I was found being walked round the local streets. My sisters all attended a convent in Edinburgh but just before my birth, my Grandfather, William Hugh Ewen, a pioneer aviator, had passed away and so there were no funds available to send me to Fettes College, which had been his plan and which would have given me a very good educational start in life.

I went to Wardie Primary School in Granton Road Edinburgh for primary education and as far as I can remember, had a wonderful time apart from the scars I still bear from collisions with a low wall in the playground, which was covered in grit. A very painful experience, especially as my fall was caused by a young lady on whom I had romantic intentions up to that point. I had an obsession with space travel and every Sunday night would sit with my mother and step-father and listened to Journey into Space on the radio and to the adventures of Captain Jet Morgan, Doc Matthews, Mitch Mitchell and Lemmy Barnett as they explored the universe. It is worth remembering that these episodes were transmitted between 1953 and 1956 and long before Sputnik orbited the Earth on the 4th October 1957.

Around that time, I had my 11+ interview with the Headmaster of Wardie Primary School along with my mother. I was asked what I wanted to do when I left school, and I explained that I wanted to be a rocket engineer, spending all my spare time at home designing rockets for trips to the moon and beyond. The word of the Headmaster still ring in my ears "You stupid boy" he said, "if God had meant man to go into space he would have given him wings" and so it was that I was selected to do a five-year Latin and French syllabus at Broughton Senior Secondary School. I did not enjoy Latin or French and soon grew to hate Mathematics as well. On my first day at school, in the Maths class, the Maths teacher, Miss McDonald called out all our names, and when she got to mine I was called out to the front of the class. "Do you have three sisters, Gillian, Annette and Sidnie?," she asked. "Yes Miss" I replied and was promptly given three of the belt on each hand just to set the record straight as they had been particularly bothersome pupils, and she wanted me to know that my card was marked. After that I had no desire to excel at Maths and once I had reached fifteen I left school as soon as possible. The only job I could find with no qualifications was as a Grass Seed Warehouseman at Robert Edgar and Sons in Mitchell Street, Leith, where Eddie the foreman took me under his wing and I was soon learning how to blend the various seeds into mixtures for tennis courts and bowling greens. To have the right mixture you blend creeping red fescue, Oregon Blue ryegrass, rape, and a variety of others, all measured in exact quantities and bagged up to be collected by the local carrier and delivered all over the UK. Each day an elderly ERF truck would pull up with the driver John Genelli and his driver's mate Peter from Sadlers Transport in its distinctive gray and maroon livery, and I would watch with envy as this team got on with loading the truck for delivery to Glasgow the next day. One day John arrived without Peter, who had just passed his Driving Test, and asked me if I wanted to be his new mate. In a flash I accepted the job and was soon in the world of road haulage. It was an interesting occupation, as we delivered what had come through from Glasgow that morning and loaded up the truck for dispatch to Glasgow that afternoon. This was before the M8 motorway between Edinburgh and Glasgow had been built, and John would leave very early in the morning with the Glasgow-bound load and pick up the Edinburgh-bound truck for delivery. We carried everything from coffins to nails used to close them, from foodstuffs to additives and went all over Edinburgh delivering and collecting.

I left Sadlers to enlist in the Regular Army, but to this day can still tie the knots to secure a load of whisky, without breaking a single bottle, and this in the days before fork lift trucks and containerised loads. It was critical not to break any bottles when loading the trucks, and these were the big rigid eight-wheel trucks which could hold thousands of cases on each load. You were allowed a fixed number of breakages per load, so you had to ensure that one of the team had the empty flasks used to capture any spilt amber liquid and another to ensure that only the set number of bottles would be damaged and the precious liquid captured. I am sure that my love of single malt whiskys comes from taking home the spoils of a well-packed load.

I have dealt with my time in the Army in a separate Chapter, so will continue with life at 61 Inverleith Row for a while. We lived at the top floor in a large three-bedroomed flat in what was called a "stair". There were three other flats in the stair, one occupied by a gentleman called Mr. Harper who shared the same birth date as Winston Churchill, Mr. and Mrs. Tom Fairlie, whose New Year's parties were legendary due to Mrs. Fairlie's habit of putting alcohol into everything, especially the devilled eggs, but was teetotal herself, and an old spinster whose betrothed had been killed on the Western Front in the First World War.

On her demise the flat was sold and the new owners turned up to redecorate what was a time warp from 1918, and on a Sunday afternoon I met Joan, their daughter, and at the age of nine I asked her out for a date: dinner in my house, and she accepted. Some fifty-seven years later we are still together, though sometimes it has been interesting. On leaving the Army we moved to Rosyth in Fife where I started work in industry, and on the 24th May 1979 we were blessed with the arrival of Claire Louise Terry, born in the Dunfermline Maternity Hospital at 08:20 and weighing in at 7 lb. 12 oz. On the 12th February 1981, Gemma Kate joined us at the same hospital at 01:20 in the morning weighing 7 lb. 12 oz. We decided after that the chances of another girl were too great, and so I got my desire of two daughters, which was honestly all I wanted. As I had become a salesman in August 1980 I spent a long time on the road often arriving home in the early evening to be met with a crying child in a pram, which I would walk round the estate until asleep so that I could creep back home to have my dinner. It was about that time that I discovered the joys of the microwave, one of the best inventions known to man!

I found being the father of daughters a great challenge, but both are now happily married and have blessed us with a Granddaughter and a Grandson, so our family is complete. More of them later, perhaps.

Chapter 2: A child of 47 (1947)

As I said in the introduction, I was born at 01:38 on the 22nd December 1947, to Juliette Lumsden Terry and Harry Fielding, so my Birth Certificate has me down as John Richard Fielding-Terry, although I have only used the name John Terry for all of my life. Lately this has been a problem due to a footballer of the same name, and I have been introduced at a conference as the man who has disappointed more Hotel receptionists! At one hotel, the receptionist had even had her hair done just for me, and had I not had my wife with me, I am sure she would have inflicted pain on me for disappointing her so much. But back to the real world. When I was about four, my mother got into a relationship with Andrew Patrick McMahon and bore him five children, one stillborn, until marrying him after the birth of my youngest brother James, and changing all their names from Terry to McMahon. By this time I was 12 and decided that I did not want my name changed and so remained a Terry, although the name referred to my mother's late husband Kenneth Sidney Terry, killed in action in Normandy on the 17th August 1944. I had a great upbringing, except for the fact that I was a boy with five sisters and eventually two younger brothers. My mother loved children and was soon involved with the Guild of Service, helping out with the care of unwanted babies being put up for adoption. Soon our house had a stream of unwanted babies passing through from three days old to three months old when they left us to go to their adoptive parents. At this time my mother was still having babies of her own, and such was the demand for her services that I can remember three cots side by side, with my youngest brother James in the middle one. Such was the love that my mother had that we soon noticed that we were getting some very poorly babies, but every one we got was handed back for adoption, glowing with health. After some 52 foster babies and with dwindling health, my mother decided to give up on the fostering and took some well-earned rest.

She never really talked about Harry, my father, until the day of my wedding to Joan, the girl next door, when she told me that I was a lot like him, in many ways, she explained briefly that times had been hard with three daughters, and that was all she could say. I knew he had been around because Gillian, my eldest sister would occasionally taunt me about him. No photos existed of him, and no mementos, so I was left with no knowledge of that side of my life.

In 2010 I decided to do some research into my maternal Grandfather, William Hugh Ewen, whom I had been told was the first Scotsman to fly and so it was that I got involved with genealogy. My first step was to contact the Museum of Flight at East Fortune as I knew that my Granddad had obtained his Brevet or Pilots Licence on the 14th February 1911 and I thought it would be great to celebrate his centenary of flight with the museum. I was soon in robust discussion with the Assistant Curator at the Museum, Ian Brown who assured me that my Grandfather was not the first and that they had no interest in celebrating his event as they had already chosen someone for that honour. So I spent several days and nights researching the first hundred pilots to have achieved a Pilot's licence in the UK, and knew that my Grandfather was number 63 in the UK but was the fifth Scot to hold a UK Pilot's licence. To work this out I had to investigate the lineage of all 100 pilots, and became very adept at working out how Family Trees work.

Soon I was working on my own tree and that of Joan my wife, and no matter how hard I looked I could not confirm the family tree of my own father, Harry Fielding. I knew he had been born in Cumbria, and had faint memories of a train journey with my mother on a steam train with the sea on my right on a trip to see a lawyer and deduced that he must have come from somewhere near Workington. A trip to Workington and research at the local newspaper and library got me no nearer, and I was about to give up in frustration and even a trip to West Register House in Edinburgh led me to believe that the only evidence of Harry Fielding's time in Edinburgh was me and a signature on my Birth Certificate. I asked all my family, but no one could come up with any information that could help me track him down.

A friend had decided to set up an organisation called The Trenchard Partnership to provide genealogical research, and so it was that I approached him to find out if he could try to identify any surviving relations of my Grandfather's business partner Andrew Mitchell Ramsay in my quest for details about the Company they had formed in Glasgow called the W H Ewen Aviation Co Ltd and asked him as an aside to see if he could track down my father, giving all the details I had accumulated over the two years. There was no luck with the business partner, but he was able to tell me that he found the Death Certificate of my father and his mother, and that the reason I could not find him was because he had changed his name to Harry Graham-Fielding, and that I had a half-brother and three half-sisters that I knew nothing about. So it came to pass that I wrote the famous "You don't know me, but I think you are my half-brother" letter that tried to answer some of my questions and to see if I could have a picture of my father.   I was delighted to get a reply that had more questions than answers, but eventually I got a picture of my dad and when I shared it with my own sisters they immediately confirmed it was him. So the search was over, and although my two half-sisters are not keen to go any further with our relationship, I have shared births and marriages with them as I do see them as part of my extended family.   I had asked my mum where the names John Richard had come from and she had no idea; she said they were definitely not from her side of the family, but when I did an extended search on ancestry.co.uk it was to find that my Great Great Grandfather was John Richard Fielding.

Chapter 3: On taking the Queen's shilling

I first applied to take the Queen's shilling by trying to join the Royal Air Force as an Armourer, but failed the entrance exam, and having visited many RAF Stations with the Air Training Corps, knew that the trade they offered me would result in learning such skills as sweeping the floor and making tea, so I decided instead to enlist into the Army and attended the Army Recruitment office where I was given a test by a Sergeant in the Royal Scots Guards. He looked at the results of the first test and shook his head, and gave me another test to do. I handed this one back, he shook his head again, and gave me a third test to complete. There was a lot of head shaking and muttering, and then he explained that he had never had anyone get 100% in one test, never mind three, and therefore he would put me down for Technician training with the Royal Corps of Signals which was exactly what I wanted. I had also enlisted in the Royal Signals TA, as a Driver Operator, but it soon became clear, having nearly killed my driving instructor whilst driving an Austin Champ, that my skills lay elsewhere. The Austin Champ was developed for the combat role and initially had a Rolls Royce four cylinder engine, but ended up too expensive and Landrover supplied the British Army with most of its four-wheel-drive light vehicles. The Champ was unusual in having no doors and so it was that I set out with my Instructor for my first driver training around Edinburgh. These were the days before seat belts, and after a while my Instructor decided we would try emergency stops. "I will say 'now', and bang the Works Ticket on the dash," he said as the signal. "Now turn left here" escaped his mouth, but I reacted on the "Now" and slammed the brakes on. He shot forward and hit his head on the windscreen wiper motor and was knocked unconscious. We were alone in the vehicle and as it had no doors, it was an interesting drive back to the TA Centre to explain that I had broken my Instructor, hanging on to him at every turn lest I lost him altogether. He came round and I got a real earful, and some days later I was transferred into the Regular Army much to the delight of my Instructor.

On the 29th March 1965 I boarded a train at Waverley Station Edinburgh bound for Darlington Station en route to Catterick Camp where we were met by Lance Corporal Sadler who soon had us on trucks headed for 11 Signal Regiment lines. On arrival there we were met by Sergeant "Dixie" Dean whom we soon learned to love and hate! Issued with our uniform and I suppose with the previous Air Cadet experience I soon settled in to basic training before moving to 8 Signal Regiment for my Trade training as a Line Technician. Line Technicians looked after the infrastructure of the Army's communication and I was trained on the dreaded Siemens T100R Teleprinter, and the "1+4 number 3". I called it the dreaded T100R because it was a beast of a machine that had a very powerful motor, and many gears and cogs and was used to transmit teleprinter data across the network. This was an electromechanical device which had to be precisely set and adjusted for it to work and our training often consisted of adjusting these machines precisely. It was on one of these sessions that I nearly met my maker, as I bent over the beast, the first twinges of appendicitis hit me and I bent double from the pain and my tie got caught up in the whirling mechanism and I was throttled. My colleague saw me go down and hit the emergency stop button and quickly cut my tie with his Army issue knife and saved my life. My next recollection was waking up in Catterick Military Hospital, without appendix, in a ward that was like something out of Monty Python.

On my left was an elderly cook who had just been circumcised, and on my right was a young Signalman Driver who had been driving a Line laying Landrover over the moors. Line laying Landovers did not have doors and the vehicle had turned over, throwing him out and rolling over his legs which had been amputated. At the end of the ward were two Spec Ops (Specialist Operators) who were trained to read Russian high speed morse code and transpose it onto teleprinters, for transmission back down the line for decryption and analysis. This was a very stressful job, and these guys tended to be based alone in very remote locations and would occasionally crack up. These two guys had cracked up big style and could only communicate in high speed morse, so every morning someone from a Spec Op course would come in to ask them what they wanted for lunch and tea and to hear the "dah dit dah dit dah dah dit dah" at eighty words a minute, was bizarre.

After my recuperation, I was too far behind my course to rejoin it and so waited for a Radio Technician Light course to commence, which I must confess I was more suited to, and it kept me away from that dreaded teleprinter. Radio Technicians Light looked after equipment designed to work up to 300 MHz and up to 300 Watts power output, so in the main were vehicle and man portable radio systems from the manpack A series, through the light vehicle B series up to the C series main vehicle communication systems in the Larkspur range. The top of the range was the D11/R230 combination which was a 300 watt HF (High Frequency) radio system which was beautifully made by the Marconi Radio Company and was a development of their Merchant Navy system. These usually lived in a truck and had to be treated with some caution as they had an HT voltage of 3,000 volts driving the main amplifier and this could take fingers off, or even kill, and so a complex series of interlocks had been designed in to protect the maintainers. More of this later.

I passed out of my trade training with flying colours and was immediately promoted to Lance Corporal, with promotion to full Corporal in one year if all went well and was posted out to be the Signals Technician at 25 Squadron Royal Engineers in Paderborn, West Germany as part of the British Army of the Rhine (BAOR). 25 Field Squadron Royal Engineers was a Combat Engineer Squadron, tasked with providing support to 4 Div RE and was based at Alanbrooke Barracks in Paderborn. I had a few days acclimatisation and then was sent out to join the Squadron which was taking part in a major NATO exercise. I was barely out of the Landrover when I was grabbed by the unit Signals Staff Sergeant, a wily old Jock engineer who grabbed me by the collar and pointed me in the direction of a Ferret Armoured Car with a dead C42 radio. Determined to show everyone I knew exactly what I was doing, I extracted my Test Set Radio and proceeded to check out the system. After a few minutes I had figured out it was the PSU (Power Supply Unit) and was about to make my announcement when Jock appeared, "get oot of the bluddy way" and proceeded to give the PSU a whack with a mallet where upon the sticking contacts in the vibratory PSU unstuck and it hummed into life. "Bluddy fairies" announced Jock and that remained my nickname for some time. Early in 1967 25 Squadron were issued with FV432 APC's (Armoured Personnel Carriers) and life became very hectic as all the vehicles had to have the full radio kit installed which consisted of a C42 and a B47 radio and all the control gear.

Life in BAOR could be interesting and at times dangerous, especially for any German civilians who got caught up in our wars. On one occasion, all the armour was moved into hides over the weekend ready for the start of the exercise on the Monday morning, it rained all weekend and as the Chieftains and FV432's moved out of the forests and up to the start line, they brought a lot of mud and leaves out with them turning the roads into skating rinks with the inevitable accidents as the civilians driving to work would come round a corner, hit the mud and then an AFV with horrific consequences. The exercise was immediately cancelled and we went into rescue mode. The main job of the Engineers was to blow up bridges, denying the enemy access and slowing him down. During exercise season the enemy were invariably the Orange forces, the good guys being Blue. In the heat of battle you always checked whether or not the main gun on the tank was pointing forwards or backwards. If it was pointing backwards, it was the good guys and if forwards, then blow the bridge and run. Many people forget that around 1960 to 1980 the threat from the East was very real and BAOR did provide a valid deterrent to invasion.

Around May 1968 the results of the Ockenden Report transferred first line support responsibility from the Royal Signals to REME and ended up with me having to choose between staying with the Royal Signals and being posted to 11 Signal Regiment, Verden, a known "bullshit" posting, or transferring to REME and so it was that I decided to transfer and was then posted to 7 Armoured Workshops at Fallingbostel. 7 Armoured boasted the longest convoy in the British Army and on a "crash out" could consist of over 123 vehicles. My vehicle was a 1952 Commer Q4 4x4 3-Ton G.S., Telecom Repair Truck of which we had four, called Mr. Ohm, Mr. Watt, Mr. Amp and Mr. Volt, and we tended to travel in the middle of this huge convoy. The vehicle weighed around 7 tons all up and towed a 5 KVA Coventry Climax Generator for mains supply. My AQMS, or Q was WOII Fred Waters and he didn't like to be in the middle of the convoy, so often we would be given the route card, which he would promptly screw up, and instead of an orderly procession, from the Advance party at the front, through all the various departments, to the Centurion ARV's (Armoured Recovery Vehicles) at the rear, we would all head to our designated "crash out" point. With so many vehicles including Landrovers, Bedford 3 Tonners, AEC 10 Tonners, mobile cranes, and sundry vehicles it took some time to transit the area around Hohne or Luneburg Heath, but with Fred navigating, we always ended up arriving first, selecting the best location, and getting the kettle on for a brew. On one occasion this backfired and Fred directed me to turn left at the next corner, which I did. The Commer had a flat out speed of 30mph, uphill or down dale it would go no faster, and everyone knew that Fred would find the fastest way so we had a stream of vehicles behind us with an AEC 10-tonner just behind. I did not know this particular road and as I swung round a corner, it was to see a bridge in front of us with a Bridge Classification rating of three tons on it. Too late to stop, and with an all up weight of over 8 tons and with Fred shouting "drive" in my ears I hit the bridge at 30mph and as I crossed it could hear the Generator bouncing up and down on the wooden planks, snapping them as we crossed. In my mirrors I could see the AEC 10 Tonner sideways on trying desperately to stop before the wrecked bridge. By the time the dust settled, we could see the best part of 123 vehicles snaking back down the route with nowhere to turn, and so it took several days to get the convoy out and turned round and back to barracks. We had been en route to lunch and so it was only Fred and I turned up. On another occasion in the deep midwinter we were due to rendezvous with a guide in a Landrover. He assured me that he had recc'd the route and so we set off through the forest along a narrow path. Suddenly I realised there were no tyre tracks in front of the Landrover and we were driving down an unchecked route and my vehicle wheel base was much wider than the Airportable Landrover in front. At that moment, I felt the nearside wheel slip off the track and the vehicle start to tip over, "Keep it going" shouted Fred and with a huge crash we were on our side at the front of another long convoy. In the back of the truck, was another Corporal Technician and as I levered the door open, it was to see him lying very still under a pile of technical manuals called EMER's. Fearing the worst, I started to clear the debris from him when he snored, muttered something and turned over. Within seconds he was out of the truck and headfirst into a snow drift, where he was soon awake. It took some hours to drag the truck on its side to a clearing where it could be pulled onto its wheels and towed away to be repaired.

7 Armoured Workshops was a major repair centre for all kinds of vehicles, and in the evenings was a paradise for a "Cab happy" driver and evenings would be spent on guard duty driving round the camp in a variety of vehicles. To guard the Workshop at night Polish Displaced Persons (PDP's) with War Dogs

patrolled the area. A War Dog is quite simply trained to go for the throat and kill, so we had a healthy respect for the PDP's and their dogs. Whenever a new guy came out from the UK he would be put on Guard Duty and would be encouraged to take a nap around the 10pm to 2am slot, which was when the PDP and his dog would appear at the Guardhouse looking for a cup of coffee and a warm. The dogs loved the Compo cheese which was a delicacy for them, the down side being it destroyed their sense of smell for some time, however the dogs seemed to know what the game was about and would gently smell and lick the ear of the sleeping Guard, who on waking up would be face to face with a "War" dog. The result was often humorous, with the dog trying to get more cheese and a terrified Guard trying to climb the walls. I left BAOR in early August 1969 and have very clear memories of watching the Moon landings when I should have been checking out.

I arrived at the School of Electronic Engineering at Arborfield in Berkshire and attended my upgrade course to be a 1st Class Telecommunication Technician, en route to becoming a Sergeant. Posted to 16 Airportable Workshops at Weyhill, Wiltshire not far from Tidworth Garrison, the role of the unit was to provide support at a moment's notice, so everything was palletised and ready for the off. We flew out to Cyprus for some training and on arrival got involved in another "war" in that the SAS had been flown in to test the security of the Sovereign Base Area at Dhekelia and at other units around the island. I had met up with some SAS Troopers at the School of Education at Beaconsfield where I had done a maths refresher, and they were on language courses. One of the duties of the Orderly Corporal was to close the NAAFI at 10 pm and many an Orderly Corporal had been found trussed to the flag pole on the main square for trying to close it on time. On my duty I was heading back to the Guardroom at ten past ten when I met the Orderly Officer who did not believe that I had closed the NAAAFI at 10, so forced me to unlock it and show him it was empty for the first time in many months at the time it should have been closed. "So how did you convince them to go to bed, and you a mere REME Corporal?," he asked, " Easy Sir," I said, " I offered to buy them all a beer" and they were so taken aback, they went to bed, so I kind of knew how to negotiate with them.

In Cyprus, the SAS "war" was due to start at 12:00 on the Saturday and we were all in the Corporals' Mess having lunch, with a number of tanned guys with short hair that we did not recognize in the room. Just after 12:00 we looked around and they had all vanished and none of us had noticed. Over the next few days the resident Infantry unit became more and more nervous as there was no sign of the SAS, until one day the Padre turned up at the Main Gate in a Mini, followed by a Saladin Armoured Car and a Saracen Armoured Personnel Carrier and on being asked for his Identity Card handed the man on the gate a lit flashbang device that promptly went "bang" and drove in, followed by the SAS who had overcome a patrol and taken over their uniforms and vehicles. Within a few minutes the camp had been taken over.

Over the next few days our two "wars" clashed and one day I was leading a patrol back in form the beach area, when we saw an ice-cream van. We had finished for the day so I stopped the patrol at the van and asked for ten 99's. "Buzz off" said the guy behind the counter, "Come on, we just want ten 99's," I said, and at that a Browning Hi-Power 9mm automatic pistol appeared on the counter and I realised it was an SAS trap for the resident infantry patrol that was heading up the beach towards us. "Give us the ice-creams and we'll just sit here, and we won't get involved with your "war", so the deal was done and as the patrol approached we wondered how one guy would manage to capture the whole patrol. "Eight cones please mate," said the Corporal, and the Browning Hi Power appeared again, and six figures rose up from under the sand where they had been hiding and soon a patrol was heading back in, this time consisting of SAS Troopers disguised as infantry and the base was rapidly re-captured.

After a few months back at Weyhill I was posted to Sharjah in the Persian Gulf and landed in Bahrein, where I would be acclimatised before heading out to close down the Tels Workshop in Sharjah. I remember landing in Bahrein about 9pm and as we left the aircraft walking into a wall of humid heat which was very overpowering, so I was glad that I had a few days to acclimatise. I was briefed on my duties by a Foreman of Signals (FoS) so once again I was under the control of the "Scaleybacks", a nickname for anyone on the Royal Signals. My job was to provide technical support to the resident infantry unit, which I think was the Cheshire Regiment, and to then close the workshops down before returning to the UK via Bahrein. It was a very interesting few months that I spent in Sharjah. Firstly it was just at the hottest part of the year, and my Tels Workshop was the only air-conditioned room in the workshop, so all the cold drinks were stored there. A knock on the door, I would slid a hatch up, an oily hand would appear and grasp the what seemed to be an ice cold bottle, there would be a sigh of pleasure and the hand would disappear. One day, the sky darkened to a deep yellowish grey colour, and clouds appeared followed by rain, we all dashed out in various stages of nudity only to return screaming and shouting in pain as a hail storm passed over the camp, and I had never experienced such pain before or since.

Next door to Sharjah was Dubai and as we could only work until around 1pm each day due to the heat, we would get a Landrover and drive to Dubai to visit the souk and to swim in Khan Creek. Khan Creek is now where the Jumeirah Beach Hotel is located, so the changes since I was there have been immense. I had another contact with what I took to be the SAS in Sharjah. There was a little civil war going on in the area and there were said to be Chinese Communist guerillas in the hills around so we were quite used to seeing RAF jets coming and going. On this particular day, I had a knock at the hatch so prepared a cold bottle of pop, only to slide the hatch up and be handed a slightly broken radio that I did not recognise. "Can you fix my radio please mate?," said the guy taking the drink in exchange. I had a quick look at the radio and quickly saw that it was way behind my capabilities as it had a 12.7mm hole through the middle. "Sorry mate, this is beyond repair," I said and his response was to encourage me to open it and have a proper look. Whilst I had a wide inventory of particularly useless spares, I had nothing that would repair this, but as he was well-tanned and short-haired and had a fairly aggressive manner about him, I got my tools out and had a quick look. As I had first surmised the 12.7mm heavy machine gun round had destroyed the internals and as I did not recognise the radio or most of its internal components, I had to confirm that I could not help him. "So what unit are you with?," I asked, for the paperwork. "Oh I am off the Beach Landing Party of HMS Fearless," he said and we walked out to his vehicle. Interestingly he clanked as he walked which I can only assume was magazines and grenades, and there sitting outside was a Pink Panther, a highly modified Landrover used by the SAS, with a neat line of 12.7mm holes down the side from front to back. We looked at each other he smiled and was off in a cloud of dust and spinning wheels, back to do battle.

I had to close down the workshop after that and sent a series of telexes back to my FoS in Bahrein, enquiring what I should do with the mountain of spares I had that did not seem to have any documentation or practical use. I received a telex telling me I did not have any spares, and what was I talking about, so one day in the mess I met up with a Trucial Oman Scout Tels Tech and asked him if he wanted some spares. He turned up with three trucks full of helpers and in an hour I did not have any spares. Imagine my horror when the next telex said: "Arriving tomorrow to inspect these spares and make a decision." The FoS took it in good humour and I was soon en route back to the UK in time for Christmas and some well-earned leave.

As I could not fit thirty days service in Northern Ireland on my return from leave to qualify for the medal, I did a lot of guard duties before being posted to 35 Central Workshops in Old Dalby, a major repair centre where I worked in the area refurbishing and repairing Signal Generators and a distance measuring device from South Africa called a Plessey Tellurometer, which gave me my first experience of microwave devices. Basically it measured the time taken for a signal to travel between two devices and was highly accurate for its time. At Old Dalby I was in charge of quite a large civilian contingent, and started to learn more and more about dealing with people from Hells Angels to ex SAS Troopers who had seen service in the Western Desert in World War 2. Whilst I was there I was promoted to Sergeant and duly reported to the RSM D B Richards, who told me to settle into the Mess that night. Unfortunately he forgot to mention my promotion to the Senior Mess Member, and after a very uncomfortable hour watching television with all eyes on me, someone approached and asked me what I thought I was doing there, as I was only a Corporal. I explained that I had just been promoted to Sergeant and was then promptly told to buy everyone a drink.

Formal Mess nights were an experience and I knew that the junior Sergeant would be expected to provide the loyal toast to Her Majesty. This honour fell to Mr. Vice, and I had been ribbed by another junior Sergeant that I better get it right on the night. I did some checking with both the RSM and the Duty Clerk, and at the appropriate time the RSM boomed out " Mr. Vice, the Queen" All eyes turned to me as I sat there, not moving, knowing that the other junior Sergeant who had given me all that ribbing was actually junior to me by four days. "Mr. Vice the Queen" boomed the RSM's voice again and my companion turned to me to encourage me to do my duty, but I looked him in the eyes and said: "Well then Mr. Vice, you'd better get on with it." Totally flustered he did his bit and a few extra guard duties, as they say, all's fair in love and war.

I left the Regular Army on the 21st December 1974 and moved with my wife to Rosyth, Fife, to work for Marconi Space and Defence Systems Ltd at Hillend to work on a series of secure communications devices which started my long career in ElectroMagnetic Compatibility (EMC), but that is a story for another chapter.

Chapter 4: Compo and beyond

Being brought up in a family with five sisters, three of whom were older and two younger, meant I was never encouraged to cook. My household tasks being mainly centered round keeping the stairs in the block of flats clean, and earning money from the earliest age possible, so by the age of 12 I was delivering milk from 0600 to 0715 and then morning papers from 0715 to 0815, and in the afternoon, delivering bread on an old delivery bike with a large wicker basket on the front that operated as a wind brake, and could make peddling home an arduous task.

From joining the Regular Army in 1965 I had no reason to learn to cook, being provided with three good meals a day, and in 1969 I re-met the girl next door, we became serious and then married and I discovered I had married a most wonderful cook, so again I had no reason to learn, so that by the age of around 55 my sole claim to culinary fame was my signature dish of Haggis Drambuie, as a starter, perfectly cooked boiled eggs and the ability to barbecue virtually everything to a charcoaled finish.

But what about Compo, I hear you ask? Compo was the staple food of the British Army, and usually consisted of a cardboard "ten-man pack" that included enough food for ten men for one day up to one man for ten days and everything, and I mean everything, you needed to survive was in tins – with the exception of a tin opener, toilet paper and a menu. There was a summer menu and there was a winter menu, and each pack included enough rations for three good meals a day including tea, coffee and sweets including bars of chocolate, all in tins. We all of course had our favourites, but it could be very depressing if all you could find was that all packs had the same letter! The food was very nutritious and most of it could be eaten cold, and to this day I still prefer my beans cold out of a tin with a spoon. Often if we were in a convoy then the bonnet would be opened and the tins of compo tied to the exhaust manifold with wire, and the time to the first stop carefully calculated – because if you left the tins there too long they tended to explode and cover the engine compartment with Irish Stew or some such culinary delight. On one such occasion we were pulling into a temporary hide when a pair of Dutch F104 Starfighters buzzed us and proceeded to beat us up, so we did an emergency egress, only to hear a few kilometres down the road the dull thuds of exploding compo. It would take several days to clean the engine bay after that and the stench could be overpowering. Quite often the cooks of the Army Catering Corps (ACC) would serve up an all-in stew opening up whatever was at hand and serving it as a hash with their infamous mashed potato, and so it was that you could have a stew with salmon, mutton, lamb, vegetable salad, sausages and bacon all out of tins in the same pot and it was often quite a weird colour, but you were so hungry, you would eat anything. My favourites were the oatmeal blocks and the rich fruit cake along with the tubes of Nestle condensed milk, squirted out of the tube into your mouth, delicious; but I suspect very bad for you.

But let's get back to the subject of real food. When I was nine I met my future wife in the stairs of the block of flats in which I lived in Goldenacre in Edinburgh. Joan's father had bought the flat next door and they were re-decorating the flat before moving in and I asked her to dinner on our first meeting and my mother had cooked "Mince and tatties". Fifty-six years later and it is still my favourite food of all time. Some fifteen years later, Joan, the girl next door and I were dating, and I would regularly drive four hundred miles on a Friday evening in my Austin Westminster A110 from Aborfield near Reading to Edinburgh to spend the weekend with Joan and every Saturday we would have lunch with her parents consisting of the infamous mince and tatties, with peaches and cream to follow. One Saturday, foolishly, I asked why we couldn't have peas in the mince, like my mum made, "Peas in the mince?" roared her dad, "Peas in the mince?", and I quickly changed the subject, but the next time I had lunch with them there were a few peas in the mince, and since then it has been the only way to have them, strange how easy it can be to change a lifetimes habits.

During my courtship we would spend our time in the Golden Egg restaurant, or the Wimpey before McDonald's came along and changed our eating habits. Occasionally we would splash out on fish and chips, eating them in the back of my new Austin Westminster A110 Mk II, which had tables in the back seats, watching BEA Hawker Siddely Tridents passing over us on their descent to Edinburgh Turnhouse airport before the new runway was built. I certainly knew how to show a girl a good time!

Compo and beyond

With all my foreign travel I have acquired a taste for many things, and it would be easy to just list them, but a brief explanation might help. If push came to shove then Currywurst mit pomfrets und mayonnaise would come top of the list, and no visit to Germany is complete without a trip to a Schell Imbis, or schnelly as we knew it in the Army. Another favourite from Germany was a trip to the Wienerwald restaurant in Paderborn for roast chicken, where the choice was simply a chicken, full, half or a quarter. I have never tasted chicken like that anywhere else in the world, and sadly I think there are very few of the Weinerwald restaurants around now. People often ask me what is the best country for food, and I would have to say that my favourites would be Germany, Italy and India, with Taiwan a close fourth. When I was being entertained by my good friend Roberto in Italy, I don't think I ever looked at a menu, just putting it down and leaving it all up to him. On one occasion, around fourteen of us were having a meal in the Hostaria Terza Carbonaia in Milan, and the speciality was a "red-hot" white stone and thinly sliced fillet steak which you cooked to your own liking on the stone. We were there with my boss, whose treat it was, senior members of our new owners, my friend Roberto and one of his staff. Everyone raved about the meal, especially the do-it-yourself meat course and my boss Ray indicated I should get the bill. I called the waiter over and he delivered the bill, Ray dropped his company credit card on the tray only to be told "No". So he got out his American Express card, only to be told no again, and it then dawned on me that they did not take plastic, which was a great problem as I had no cash and I knew for certain that Ray had none either. We looked at each other and at that Roberto pulled a huge wad of lire from his pocket, counted out a pile, and looked at me before smiling and saying that he would not trust a Scotsman to pay the bill again, to much hilarity.

I travelled many times in India, criss-crossing the country and usually staying at up-market International hotels, where there would always be a choice of three restaurants, usually a regional Indian one, a regional Chinese one and a European one, but I would never eat in the European one preferring to sample the Indian and Chinese food. My host and colleague was a vegetarian, so the rule was three days vegetarian and four days carnivore, and I used to look forward to every day as I knew something different would appear on the table. In all my travels in that amazing country, apart from hurting my leg in Madras,

Compo and beyond

I was never ill, especially not from any sickness and diarrhoea, and I put that down to my making a point of never rinsing my toothbrush under a running tap, always using two glasses of bottled water, one for rinsing and one for gargling.

As I have grown older my palate has changed and I now love very spicy food, but there was a time when I could not eat anything with a hint of spice. I was travelling in the USA with my boss and a senior colleague and we had arrived in Dallas, Texas where we were to spend the weekend. Our host was my very good friend Larry Tucker, and on the Saturday he took us to South Fork Ranch, the set of the TV series Dallas, and from there to his favourite Mexican restaurant. I must confess that I was very concerned about eating Mexican food due to my intolerance to spice, but Mike the boss was very keen so I asked Larry to order me the mildest, coolest dish that he could and he explained that the menu rated from Number 1, cool, to Number 12, volcanic, and so Julian and I went for No 1 whilst Mike went for No 12 despite some warnings from our host. In the afternoon we attended a barbecue and in the evening returned to the hotel where Julian and I found seats by the bar and were introduced to the Banana Banshee cocktail, whose main ingredients included ice cream, cream and banana liqueur and seemed to have a calming effect on our stomachs. Mike however continued to party and enjoy the bourbon. Around 5 am I awoke knowing that I had to get to the toilet – and fast. The burning sensations were indescribable, the end result of the "mild" Mexican lunch I had consumed. Unable to settle, I dressed and went down into the lobby where I found Julian, who was in a similar state to me, having had a very uncomfortable night. "I wonder how Mike is?," I asked, only to be told that he had been taken to a local Medical Centre during the night with what appeared to be third degree burns to his nether regions. Since then I have always followed the advice of my hosts.

Whilst I was attending a Sales Conference in Hawaii I had noticed that our hosts, who worked for a Taiwanese company, seemed to struggle with the US cuisine, and had a problem with what were, to them, huge portions, and I saw that many plates went back unfinished. We were a truly international group with people from Korea, South Africa, Australia, Canada and many other countries so on our last day together we were taken up into the hills to a

Compo and beyond

Chinese restaurant, where it turned out that apart from myself and our hosts and one or two other people, no one could use chopsticks, and no knives and forks were offered.   No problem, so we tucked in, but our hosts were only taking small portions and seemed to want to teach the other guests how to use chopsticks. Most gave up and used them as a spear – not a good solution with rice.   Politely the guests expressed themselves full, whereupon our Taiwanese hosts descended on the remains like a cloud of locusts until every plate was clear and we were given a lesson on how to eat with a bowl and chopsticks.

Have I ever been offered a plate of something I couldn't eat? Yes; once in Leeds I was offered a bowl of chitterlings, another word for tripe. and had to decline.

Chapter 5: Aviation

My first memories of aviation were as my mother bought me Dinky Toy aircraft, and I had soon acquired quite a fleet, this must have been about 1951, and I remember visiting Harburn Hobbies in Leith Street to look into the window and to choose the next addition. I was also a keen collector of Frog Spot-On aircraft and these were bought from a shop in Chambers Street, near the Museum which I loved to visit. Soon I became an avid collector of Airfix models, starting with the Supermarine Spitfire. With all this interest in aviation it was only a matter of time before I enlisted into 142 (2nd) Edinburgh Squadron Air Training Corps on the 13th December 1961, under the command of Flight Lieutenant John Syme, an ex-Bomber Command Navigator. He was a great guide and mentor and always had some sage advice to offer. One day, lost on the Pentland Hills training area, I bumped into Flt Lt Syme who asked what I was up to. "I'm lost sir" I said, "Ah young Terry, man is never lost, he is just unsure of his current location" he said. Wise words indeed, and I have never been lost since, just unsure!

The ATC was a superb organisation and offered a range of challenges and adventures to youngsters of all ages. Drill, weapons training with a Lee Enfield .303 rifle, weekend air experience flights, glider training and annual camp. My very first flight was on the 3rd July 1962 in a Vickers Varsity at RAF Topcliffe, an old WW2 bomber base and home at the time to navigational training units for the V Bomber crews. The Varsity was a successor to the Wellington bomber and had crew stations for the trainee navigators and a bomb aimer's position in the belly and some rudimentary seats for us cadets, and this flight was a four hour training mission. It soon became apparent that we had some cadets on board who were prone to air sickness and this was not a good place to be unwell, cramped, and noisy and with poor sanitation facilities there was soon a queue of white faced cadets lining up. This was great because it gave the cadets who were not prone to sickness more time in the cockpit with the pilot, enjoying the view. There became such a crowd at the rear of the aircraft with the turbulence that soon the co-pilot had to go back and order everyone back to their seats as the aircraft was becoming unstable. My friend then had to sit with his sick bag, containing his false tooth until we could land and he could rinse out the contents and recover his tooth. The joys of flying.

Aviation

In 1962 the Forth Road Bridge was being built and with Air Experience flights from Turnhouse aerodrome, near Edinburgh, it was good to get a bird's eye view of the building of the bridge. These flights could also result in some aerobatics and flying the aircraft, a great experience. In 1963, annual camp was at RAF Gaydon, an Operational Conversion Unit equipped with Vickers Valiant and Handley Page Victor V Bombers. This was a great camp, however the Victors and Valiants sortied out between 5pm and 9pm and returned to base between 10pm and 2am so sleep became at a premium. As a Senior Cadet I was offered the chance to fly in a Valiant and thus had to go into the chamber where they reduced the pressure to ensure that you were medically fit to fly, and having successfully passed that, our names went into a hat and my luck ran out. In some ways I am glad it did because that night, the winning cadet, who had made my life a misery all afternoon, was strapped into the jump seat of a Valiant, which, as it climbed away from the airfield suffered a "training" engine failure and had to circle for seven hours until all the fuel was expended and it could land again. I am not sure how I would have coped with six hours of flying in a circle, and was glad that I had lost out. Air Experience flights at RAF Gaydon were in an old Avro Anson TX155 in which over three hours were spent in the air, and I have recollections of landing at a large airbase in South Wales where Avro Shackletons were located. Another trip was to a Thor Missile site somewhere near Norfolk, and this was probably whilst attending Annual Camp at RAF Watton in 1964 which was home to two English Electric Canberra squadrons and a squadron of the Vickers Varsity in which we had another flight. By the time I left the ATC on the 1st August 1964 I had flown ten times in powered aircraft, secured my Proficiency Gliding Standard by soloing three times on the 31st May 1964 following 31 training flights in Sedburgh and Mark III gliders at 662 Gliding School at RNAS Arbroath, and had visited a diverse range of RAF bases and camps. I left the ATC as having secured my Advanced Training Badge, and, knowing that I could not join the RAF in my chosen field having failed the necessary exams for Junior Tech entry, I needed a new challenge, enlisting into a Royal Signals TA unit on the 5th January 1965 and transferring into the Regular Army on the 29th March 1965.

With the Army, I got to fly in a wide range of aircraft mostly on trooping flights, sometimes with RAF Transport Command, and sometimes on commercial flights and sometimes on air trooping flights in commercial aircraft. In the RAF all personnel flew facing the back of the aircraft, for safety reasons and I spent some hours flying to and from postings and detachments in Germany, Cyprus, Bahrain and Sharjah. Hawker Siddely Tridents, Vickers VC10's, BAC 1-11's, Armstrong Whitley Argosy's and an occasional Boeing 727 transported me to various destinations and often through active airbases with operational aircraft to look at. I left the Regular Army in 1974 and re-enlisted into the Territorial Army (Volunteer Reserve) and flew out to Germany on Lockheed Hercules aircraft a couple of times. It was possible to visit the cockpit on occasion, and the view from a Hercules is quite magnificent.

On leaving HM Forces and moving into industry, I started to travel a lot between Edinburgh and Heathrow and Gatwick, often travelling on the BAC 1-11's of British Caledonian and the Vickers Viscounts and Vanguards of British European Airways. B Cal were the preferred carriers due to the superb breakfasts, served by the Air Hostesses in their kilts, but the HS Tridents had their moments with their Auto-land capability where they could land with more or less no visibility and the possession of a Cat IIIb tie was the ultimate prize. The old Turnhouse airfield with the approach over the city could be quite hairy at times with the winds coming off the Pentland Hills and I remember more than one flight where looking out the right hand windows you got a clear view of the runways as you crabbed in on the approach. Between 1980 and 1984 I rarely flew, and then moved into a Sales career that eventually saw me crisscrossing the globe from Norway in the North, Hawaii in the West, South Africa in the South and South Korea in the East, on one trip taking thirteen flights in thirteen days and flying home on Friday 13th in Row 13, that surely should have deserved an upgrade.

From a very early model Boeing 737 from Madras to Bangalore, which had no overhead storage and seats crammed in for smaller passengers than myself, to travelling back from Lisbon to London on Concorde, which was a very memorable flight on the 27th March 1992 I travelled extensively, once calculating that in one year I had flown 126 flights with over 173 days out of the UK. The net result was a British Airways Gold Card, which whilst never getting me an upgrade, got me onto more flight decks, remembering that this was pre 9/11. Once on the flight deck, and after chatting with the pilots about the effect of electronic equipment on flight, I invariably was invited to stay for the landing, strapped in, with headphones on just enjoying the view. The best ever was during the time that BA were introducing the Boeing 777 into the fleet and most flights were between London and Paris, allowing pilots and to practice operating the aircraft. Because this was such a short hop, I was strapped in before take-off and enjoyed the whole flight from the best seat in the house. An early morning arrival into London on a Boeing 747-400 approaching over the city was memorable as was an early morning arrival into Istanbul. I managed a cockpit visit on every aircraft BA was operating, except Concorde between 1990 and 1999, and never got tired of watching the professionalism of the crews.

Flying gave me the opportunity to practice my favourite hobby, people watching, and airports and aeroplanes are just the best place to indulge in that occupation. I had a policy of never asking for an upgrade, because then anyone could say no, and you had the embarrassment of knowing that everyone in the queue behind you knew you had been unsuccessful, so it was better to get a comfortable seat and watch all the different techniques in trying and failing to get that upgrade. On one memorable flight to Istanbul, I was near the back of Economy sitting in the aisle seat when the husband in the seat next to me, after much huffing and puffing from his wife, demanded that they be moved into Club Class as her seat was faulty. The Purser, a charming lady, explained that the flight was full, and that she would be unable to locate two Economy seats together, so I moved out so she could check the seat, which appeared to be perfectly serviceable. After a few minutes, as we neared departure, he tried again, he could see two empty seats in Club, it was a long flight and they should be moved. I should say here that on every flight I have ever taken, I make a point of saying hello to the cabin staff as I board the aircraft, and often ask them how they are before they can greet me, and as I take my seat, I always chat to any staff around, that means that as they start to dispense any drinks, they invariably remember that nice man who said hello, and you often get two! The Purser approached with the drinks trolley and the lady had an orange juice, and the gentleman got a red wine, and I got two Vodkas and Slim Line tonics. At the meal service, I asked for a white wine, and got two, my companions only getting one each, but it had been noted and comments made. I had got into conversation with a Russian lady across the aisle, who had noticed all the commotion and it was agreed that we should enjoy an after dinner drink, so I went back to the galley and returned with two malt whiskies and two Baileys with ice. As I settled down into my seat, the hand shot up to the crew call button, and the Purser appeared, "I would like two whiskies and two brandies please," he said. "I am terribly sorry, but this gentleman just caught me as I closed the bar, and it is now locked" and walked off with a smile. The moral of the story, always be nice to the cabin crew, they always win in the end.

We were in Bruges on holiday when 9/11 happened and flying changed forever. Nowadays, the fun and adventure seems to have gone, I still make a point of greeting the cabin crew, and now they might just chat to you for a moment, no more visits to the flight decks, no more upgrades, just low prices and small cramped seats, definitely the Golden age of flying is over for me.

Chapter 6: And into industry

One of the benefits on leaving the Army was to get a Resettlement course and I elected to take mine at my new employers, Marconi Space and Defence Systems Ltd (MSDS) and as I had joined the Company as an incoming skilled worker I was entitled to a subsidized flat with the Scottish Special Housing Association (SSHA). I had secured this job to work as a Post Design Services Engineer (PDS) on a range of secure communications equipment called BIDs, at the time a classified acronym, and my future boss during my interview had asked me what the letters stood for, which I had declined to answer on national security grounds. He told me he would employ me and then I would have to tell him, and it was with much pleasure that on my starting my new job, he asked me again and again I declined on the basis of "need to know".

Of course now we have Wikipedia, I can confirm that it stood for British Internal Departmental, but it was a source of annoyance that I would not share the definition with him. Dave was ex Royal Air Force as were a number of my colleagues including Stuart Allen, who had a quite brilliant mind and was often designing and building such things as a Teletext decoder that was only just being transmitted. I was responsible for the PDS work on three BID devices and this soon brought me into close working with CESG an offshoot of GCHQ and I met a great mentor in the person of Ken Foulkes who soon educated me in the black magic that was ElectroMagnetic Compatibility (EMC). With Ken's help and guidance I was soon able to solve all sorts of problems on the equipment and I found out that duties of a PDS engineer could be many and varied, from the colour of the paint, to why the connectors regularly broke on the BID 150, and to why the cards always fell out of a particular device during transit. I became adept at solving everyone else's problems and made a number of trips to sensitive locations to fix things that were broken. On one occasion I had to visit the Cabinet Office in London and was directed to enter through Downing Street, long before the barriers were erected, and was saluted in by the duty Bobby and back out again. The unit I had been sent to fix had a recurring fault, which I knew could be easily fixed, and if it ever got out just how easy it was to fix, then my exotic trips would soon end. I was escorted to the relevant room and insisted that my escort leave the room due to the Secret nature of the equipment, did the fix that involved no more than the use of a pencil eraser, waited fifteen minutes then knocked on the door to be taken back to the car, the unit working perfectly in the rack. The Design Authority was in Portsmouth and we had regular meetings and visits to the Browns Lane facility, and on occasion would transfer classified modules to and fro for repair and modification. These modules had to be locked in a briefcase which was chained to one of our party's wrist by the Security Controller, and the key handed to another unidentified member of the party. On arrival at the airport, we presented a letter to the Security point that explained that we had no access to the contents, but they were inactive and posed no risks. Sometimes it worked, and other times we had a difficult crew on, and the exchange went something like this:

"Open the case, sir."

"I am sorry I do not have a key, it is in Hillend in Scotland."

"Well put it through the X-Ray machine." (this with it still strapped to my wrist).

"No thanks, can you get the pilot please?"

Then the pilot would arrive and ask us what was inside.

"I cannot tell you, but it is non-operational and contains no hazards."

At that we were usually let on with instructions to the stewardesses to deck us if we tried to leave our seats!

Ministry meetings were usually great fun, with long discussions taking us nowhere, but these devices were critical to the security of the nation, but sometimes it would all get too much and a break for tea and coffee would be called. I was always intrigued that as the teas and coffees arrived, Bernard, the Project Manager, would ask a really obtuse question that would be immediately addressed by the assembled group, wink at me and we would serve the teas and coffees making sure we got the best biscuits. As we finished, Bernard would ask what was being discussed, say that it was irrelevant and take the meeting back over. A "red herring" delivered and recovered with great skill and dexterity.

The PDS Contract for the equipment expired, and I found myself with the choice of working on the GWS Sea Dart guided missile system, or the Clansman radio and as neither appealed to me, I looked elsewhere and saw

And into industry

that Ferranti at Robertson Avenue in Edinburgh were looking for a senior PDS Engineer. I was interviewed and offered the job, but I had stressed during my interview that I did not want to work on radar, as it was too clunky and mechanical for me. And so it was that on my first day at Ferranti I was introduced to the Blue Parrot radar as fitted to the Hawker Siddely Buccaneer. Not what I had planned, but my day was about to get much worse when I met my new boss, who had been in the US for training at the time of my interview. He was ex-RAF and his first words filled me with doom:

"I don't like you, you're ex-Army."

I explained to him that it was not what I was then, but what I could do for him now that mattered, but he left me in no doubt that I was inferior and not to be trusted. I actually worked on a neat bit of kit called the GPIC (Ground Position Indicator/Corrector) which allowed the navigational system on the Buccaneer to be corrected in flight with just one swing of the radar to locate pre-set waypoints. Based on a new military grade microprocessor it was a very complex and clever item that gave the crews the ability to fly at very low level at night over West Germany. The Buccaneer had initially been designed for the Royal Navy, to fly at very low level under the radar and to attack Russian cruisers by tossing their bombs in an arc in a very complex maneuvere. With the cancellation of TSR 2 and the F111 the RAF had to adopt the Buccaneer for its low level attacks in Germany and we had RAF crews visit us to tell us of the absolute faith they had in GPIC as they hurtled across Germany at under 500 feet at 500 knots, flying under power lines and depending on GPIC to tell them where the pylons were. Scary!

My relationship with my boss did not improve, and on one occasion my quality of soldering was ridiculed in front of the department. I was annoyed at this as I had won a prize in my Army training, and what I had done that day had been in my opinion, some of my best work. So I went to see the Chief Instructor and asked him to inspect my work, which he passed as perfectly acceptable, so I asked him to re-work the part, which he did. I took the part back to my boss; he took one quick glance at it, and declared it rubbish once again. I then turned over the inspection card and showed him the Chief Inspector's stamp and knew at that moment I needed to find another job – and soon. As it happened, MSDS, my old employer, realised just what a valuable asset I was and I was soon heading back to Hillend – but not before I got my

And into industry

final revenge. Due to my TA service with the Intelligence Corps, I always made sure that the resident Security Controller was aware of the skills and abilities I had, and would always spend time at their office swapping stories. One of my skills was the ability to change the settings on the MoD standard combination lock, and I was in possession of a key to do so. I knew my boss had lax security over the combination of his safe, which contained secret documentation, so on my last day whilst he was at lunch, I opened the lock and changed the combination to my birth date, having first told the Security Controller of my plan. On return from his lunch, he tried to open the cabinet to no avail. After a couple of attempts I asked him what the problem was, and he told me the lock was faulty, so I dialed in my combination, opened the lock and promptly shut it again. He looked at me in amazement, and so I repeated my actions, locking it once again. His hand shot out, grabbed the telephone and called the Security Controller to his office to have me arrested for breaking into a secure safe. On his arrival, the Security Controller asked me how I had opened it in the first place. "I used the combination he wrote down on the back of his desk blotter," I said, packed my bag, said my goodbyes and left Ferranti for good.

I returned to my work at MSDS in Hillend, but in June 1980 I was approached by a Sales Manager of a company called MCP Electronics Ltd Wembley, and asked if I fancied a career in sales. I gave it some thought and agreed to meet the MD, a gentleman called Svenn Davidsen, at the Scotelex Electronics Show at Ingleston, near Edinburgh and had a very interesting interview. And so it was that on the 1st August 1980 I became a Field Sales Engineer selling a wide range of high-technology materials, mainly in the defence and computer industry in Scotland and Ireland. Ron Adams was the Sales Manager, and he told me just to get on with learning how to sell and they would send me for formal training at a later date. I took to technical sales like a duck to water, and soon had a stream of colleagues heading north to help me learn about the complexities of selling such complex components to a burgeoning industry in Silicone Glen and Southern Ireland. We covered a wide range of products from little pieces of bent metal made by a company called Thermalloy Inc in Dallas to conduct heat away from delicate electronic components, through EMC gaskets made by Chomerics and later by Tecknit, both in the USA to very high performance radio frequency (RF) power amplifiers to motors used to drive the windscreen wipers on Chieftain Main Battle Tanks, a very wide range of products and customers.

During that time I met some very good people from whom I learned a lot, both technically and commercially, and travelled far and wide flaunting my wares. Negotiation skills were honed, and I soon learned to be able to barter and successfully convinced two major customers, Burroughs Machines of Cumbernauld and IBM of Spango Valley, to do business with the Distributor rather than the manufacturer, because we were more flexible, could hold stock and were able to respond at a moment's notice. On one occasion the President of Thermalloy, Bill Jordan, came to visit his main customer as he had seen all the sales drop off. We were travelling with his new UK Managing Director, and as I was driving to the customer. I tried to explain to Bill that I was the reason for his drop in orders with the customer, but that he could see an increase in sales with MCP for the same materials. This was so unusual that even after the customer had explained to Bill what an excellent job we were doing, he was still arguing with me as we drove back, so I pulled into a Little Chef, which was empty, and we carried on a very robust discussion much to the horror of the new MD. Eventually he realised what I had achieved and called the waitress over. "Get the Scotsman some Apple pie and Ice Cream" he roared, being an ex US Marine Corps Lieutenant Colonel. Not to be outdone, I said "and get a portion for this damn Yankee", at which he exploded, "I'm not a damn Yankee, I am a Louisiana man," and stormed out. It seemed I had mortally offended him without knowing it, and the new MD Brian, sat there with his head in his hands moaning that he was about to be fired. It was a very quiet journey back to the airport. Later when I visited Thermalloy in Dallas with two colleagues someone asked me if I was the person who had called Bill a damn Yankee, and I said I was, was told: "Boy, you only have one life, be careful with it" and everyone laughed. At Thermalloy in Dallas I met my very good friend Larry Tucker who was the International Vice President of Sales, someone whom I thought was just the most professional salesman I have ever met. Larry had a wicked sense of humour and was a past master at wind-ups, spending some time creating exactly the right environment for the best effect. We spent the weekend in Dallas, being taken to a speciality steak restaurant that was famous for cutting off the ties of anyone stupid enough to wear one, and we had all been told that the dress code was ties, so why were we the only ones wearing them? Attractive cow-girls duly arrived with shears and three more ties were pinned to the rafters. The menu was all about huge lumps of meat and the ultimate was the Bull-shipper, a 42oz cut of prime US beef, then the Cowboy. I chose the Cowgirl, a 28oz mesquite charcoal-cooked steak, and to this day I am sure it was the best steak I ever ate. It was so good that I noticed a small piece of meat stuck to the bone and with no-one looking, picked it up, and nibbled. Bill Jordan spotted this and immediately called for another as I was obviously still hungry, but I managed to stop it just in time. Unfortunately, I had made quite an impression on Larry and some weeks later he met a fellow American who wanted to set up a Scottish operation to fund the buying back of Dunstaffnage Castle, acquired from the Clan MacDougalls in the 15th century by the Campbells. Stuart Jeffrey McAlpine was a supposed self-made millionaire who was keen to set up a venture in Scotland and at our first meeting I became a Director and shareholder in S J Mac Ltd. We bought a car, we rented a factory unit and he gave me £10,000 pounds to get the venture started, and so it was that I left MCP Electronics and started to wheel and deal in electronic components with his US company. A trip to the US introduced me to his partners, and then in the April 1985 I travelled alone to the US to negotiate new franchises and suppliers. It was then I learnt that all was not as it seemed, and so on my return, it was to find out that I had been sacked, and my wife and my secretary joined me. It was a great shock and it was five weeks before I was back in full-time employment, this time working for Manhattan Skyline in Maidenhead, another supplier of electronic components to an ever-changing industry. Manhattan Skyline was quite unusual in that it had five Directors, all equal, and a Sales meeting could be quite a dynamic and career-wrecking event, so lessons on presentation were quickly acquired and a very accurate grasp on what was going on in your territory became critical. After some time, I was asked to move to Maidenhead, and so it was that Joan and I and the girls moved from Rosyth to Thame, a culture shock as both my daughters had broad Fife accents and used different words to describe things such as baffies instead of slippers. But children are very adaptable and they soon were able to converse with the people of Thame.

We represented mainly Japanese and Taiwanese suppliers, and on one occasion I was sent to a Sales Conference in Hawaii, which was a great experience. I also did a lot of trade with Amstrad on components on its PCW word processing systems, and heaven help you if you were late delivering to the

And into industry

factories, Alan Sugar having a very keen interest in anything that was late. On one occasion whilst visiting Amstrad Towers, I was standing near the door and saw Alan Sugar approaching. I opened the door to him and he asked: "Who are you?"

"John Terry, sir, Manhattan Skyline."

He responded in very unflattering tones, much to the delight of all the other salesmen in the reception area. On my return to base I told my boss that I had met Alan Sugar, and when I told him what he had said, he to roared with laughter.

In 1988 I was approached by an old colleague who asked me if I wanted to get back into the EMC business full time and I jumped at the chance, joining Chomerics Europe in Marlow as a Field Sales Engineer on the emigration of George Nash to Australia. I knew I wanted to go into international sales, and following some changes I became Regional Sales Manager, Europe and then Distribution Sales Manager. Both roles I thoroughly enjoyed, and travelled from Norway in the North, to California, USA in the West, to Korea in the East and South Africa in the South, selling and teaching and lecturing wherever I went. It is impossible to say where my favourite was, but I have many friends all over the globe with whom I still keep in touch.

In 1999 I was head-hunted to join one of my old Distributors, HITEK Electronic Materials Ltd, in Scunthorpe, and spent 13 happy years moulding it into an award-winning company that enjoyed 13 years of continuous growth. In December 2012 I retired from running the Company, having handed over to the new MD, Jim Lawton, who has carried on the good work by winning another prestigious award for Business Excellence. Now I run Argent Vulpes Ltd (AVL) set up to provide SME's with a support service to allow them to do business with the major defence and aerospace sub-contractors.

Chapter 7: The Innovation Era

This all started with a phone call to my company HITEK, from the then Assistant Harbourmaster of the Port of London, who had remembered seeing a radar-absorbing shroud on the main masts of the Royal Navy's Type 42 Destroyers during his time in the Falklands Island campaign on the St Galahad, lost in the Bluff Cove disaster. He wanted to know if we were able to make a radar-absorbing shroud on a much larger scale, around 80 metres tall, due to navigation issues around the Kentish Flats Wind Farm that was affecting navigation caused by ghosting and phantom wind farms showing up on ships' radars. My first reaction was no, not only on the impossibility using current technology, but also from a cost aspect. I was due to fly out of London Heathrow for a ten-day business trip to the USA so decided to visit Roy at his office in Gravesend, Kent where he shared with me some amazing images of phantom radar returns from imaginary wind farms and so even though I assured him that there was no current solution, I would think about the problem.

My journey took me to several interesting companies in the US, and as I met and talked with various people manufacturing a diverse range of products from corrosion-controlling additives to creating electrically-conducting fabrics of conductive materials, by the time I returned to the UK I knew how to solve his problems in a cost effective manner. I had brought back some conductive thread as a sample for a new generation of wound dressings and went with one of my Business Development Mangers to a company called Pera Innovation in Melton Mowbray, where we had an interesting meeting. During this meeting we were joined by a gentleman called Andrew Jones, who after some time, asked me if I would be good enough to draw on the board my concept for a solution to an issue or problem I had. To say I was taken aback would be an understatement, as I had not discussed this with anyone, so I soon had my concept on the board.

"Right" said Andrew, "I can get you three million Euros to develop that," and the funding issue had gone away. Sadly even though we came up with a very good technical solution to "stealth" Wind Turbine towers, we did not get the funding as it was thought it could be used to stealth a boat to sail up the Thames and blow up Parliament. Sadly this could not happen as it would be the wrong radar band that would be stealthed. Another bid for Technology Strategy Board funding was more successful, and soon the Safe Passage consortium had been formed and all the issues from developing a new low cost Radar Absorbing Material (RAM) to developing the techniques needed to mount massive RAM panels onto Wind Turbines over 100 metres high on land, or in the sea were soon developed.

Around this time I was invited to attend an even called HybridMat at the Royal Aeronautical Club in London, and must selfishly admit that the main reason for going was to see if their acclaimed Library had any mention of my Grandfather, William Hugh Ewen, the pioneer Scottish aviator. During one of the sessions a slide was put up and suddenly I knew that I could not only stealth the Wind Turbine towers, but I also knew how to stealth the blades. There is a significant difference in the issues between marine radar and aviation radar in that marine radar is looking at slow moving targets such as land, islands and other ships, whereas aviation radar is looking for fast moving targets. The lightning strike conductors in the wind turbine blades are large lumps of metal, and as the tips of the blades travel at around 300 knots on a windy day, the effect on aviation radar can be quite dramatic. The slide that I saw answered so many questions and I was soon back with my friends at Pera Innovation and the BladeRunner project was born. As an aside I obtained a catalogue of my Grandfather's business from the library, so all in all made very successful visit.

Both the Safe Passage and the BladeRunner projects were seen through to successful conclusions in that sample materials were produced and tested but neither ever made it into production. From early on we realised in both our consortiums that there was a lack of support at higher levels arising from a refusal to believe that a small company solving other people's problems in Scunthorpe could have come up with solutions that had defeated major defence companies. Furthermore, with the development of low-cost masking solutions such as ShadowMaker and SpacerRAM there was a reluctance by the Ministry of Defence to trial our solutions. On one famous day, we delivered a ShadowMaker panel to RAF Spadeadam, but there was so little interest that we left it in the car and brought it home!

The innovation era

I often say that you can quickly see if someone has an innovative mind by asking them if they are on one side of a hill and you are on the other, how many different solutions are there for getting to you, you would be amazed as to how many people will immediately say one. But there can be many more ways than that; how many can you come up with? With innovation, invariably the major stumbling block is investment. You can come up with the perfect mousetrap, but if you don't have the funds to patent it and develop it, then like many great ideas it will shrivel and die. My latest invention can massively cut the energy usage of hotel kitchens worldwide, cut food waste, reduce stress and anxiety in the mornings, but will be very unlikely to make it into production due to the high costs of patenting it, and finding a partner to manufacture and distribute it. Intrigued? then get in touch and sign a Non-Disclosure Agreement (NDA) and perhaps we could talk.

Chapter 8: Serving the community

I have always had the desire to put something back into the communities I have lived in, and have served in the Royal Observer Corps, been an emergency driver in the dead of winter, been in Junior Chamber International, and been a Thame Lion. I have trained to be a public speaker, and worked for ten years in a Breed Rescue charity and am now planning to be a Business Mentor for the Prince's Trust.

I think it is the responsibility of everyone to put something back into their communities, but I feel that I am very much in the minority. When I left the Regular Army in 1974 I needed to have a hobby that would put something back and so I chose the Royal Observer Corps (ROC). I was stationed at RAF Pitreavie Castle and my job was to plot the locations of nuclear explosions reported through to us by the network of listening posts scattered throughout the UK. These underground posts were able to determine the point of detonation of ground or air nuclear explosions should the country come under attack from the Soviets. I stood behind a large glass panel with a map of the UK stencilled on it, and taking a piece of teleprinter tape, read the tape and put a sticker on the map of a mushroom cloud, with red for an air burst and green for a ground burst and an indication of the location and size of the blast. Then, given the wind directions, we would plot the plume of radioactive contamination and this would allow the people on the other side of the glass wall to direct the responses of the rescue and emergency services accordingly. To this day I still have the ability to write backwards as quickly as most people can write normally. At one exercise I was busy plotting a string of bombs over the UK and had just finished my last one when there was a furious knocking from the other side of the glass. I looked up to see a senior naval officer pointing at my last placement and shaking his head, indicating that I had made a mistake. I checked the tape, nodded and gave him a thumbs-up, indicating a good plot. Another furious banging and I asked my controller to confirm my plot which he did and we both gave the thumbs-up. The naval officer was unhappy, so our Shift Leader was called and he confirmed the accuracy of the plot, at that the officer appeared from behind the screen and asked if we were certain that no mistake had been made and we assured him that a 40 Megaton nuclear device had detonated several hundred feet above our heads. So he asked what exactly that meant, and we gently explained that he was actually at the bottom of a very radioactive hole in the ground and we were all dead. "Well that's ruined everything," he said and stormed off in a huff. As a perk I was issued with a Home Office "get out of jail free" card that had to be carried at all times. If there was a national emergency with the likelihood of a nuclear attack, my job was to rush to the Pit and man my post and the card ensured that I could pass any checkpoint without let or hindrance and without excuse. You have to realise that holding that card allowed access only to me and not my family, and I hoped that I would never have to choose between staying with my family and descending into the safety of the Pit. On one occasion my boss at Marconi Space and Defence Systems spotted the card and asked what it was for and I explained the significance. He was amazed that I would be admitted and not him and his family, but I tried to explain that it was a sacrifice I thought I should make. His next question left me bemused when he asked me to get him a family card the next time I was on duty, as he felt he was much more important than me to be saved.

I also joined the Junior Chamber International (JCI) which exists to promote the ethos of young people between the ages of 18 and 40 to take "collective action to improve themselves and the world around them." Some of the time was spent on meetings and discussions but in or around 1976 we were asked to help provide the drivers for the Gathering of the Clans in Edinburgh, driving vehicles provided by the then British Leyland. There was a complete range of cars including Range Rovers, a prototype Rover SD1, Mini's and so on. I had the privilege to drive the Rover prototype, and on one occasion was tasked to pick up a young lady from her hotel and deliver her to a function. I was allocated the Range Rover, as I was used to driving large four-wheel drive vehicles in my time in the Army. I duly turned up at the hotel to be met by the young lady wearing a very figure-hugging full length cocktail dress in which she was unable to step up into the high vehicle. After some minutes we figured out that if I bent right down, and she stepped onto my hands I could lift her up and onto the seat, and she would be able to swivel round allowing us to get to the function just in time. Getting out was just as complicated and I was glad that there were no Press photographers around at the time. I also made sure that someone else drew the short straw when the time came to pick her up and return her to her hotel, and she sent a very kind note thanking us for our deeds. It was great fun to be able to drive all these vehicles around and to support the Gathering. On another occasion we entered a team into Chamber Challenge run by the famous Donnie B McLeod, and travelled up to Sutherland for an on-air challenge but we were narrowly beaten.

On moving to Thame in 1986 I became involved with the Lions Club of Thame and became a Thame Lion. Lions are an international organisation and use the precept "We serve" as its motto. I had a great time as a Lion, taking on the roles of PR and Fund Raiser and was very successful in getting the Lions into nearly every edition of the Thame Gazette, the local newspaper. I was so successful that one day I was visiting the offices of the Thame Gazette, when the door burst open and a representative of an alternative organisation came in dressed up in drag as part of a fund raising campaign to complain that the Lions were getting too much publicity. He didn't notice the Editor and I sitting there, had a rant at the receptionist and flounced out slamming the door after him. There was a stunned silence, we looked at each other and burst out laughing and I was able to convince him not to do an article on the strange lady, bad mouthing the Lions.

Getting money for charity is always a challenge, and we often planned events a year in advance to raise funds for a Guide Dog puppy or for equipment for a needy family or to help someone with mobility issues and I spent a lot of time negotiating with local businesses for prizes for raffles and sponsorship. We also planned a Beaujolais Nouveau run and we were able to get the loan of two cars from local garages to allow us to drive to Villefranche-sur-Saone where we met up with other French Lions Clubs who were very good hosts. On one outing we met a young French girl who had travelled to Harefield Hospital for a heart and lung transplant, the costs of which had been met by some of the Lions Clubs we met in France and we and several other UK Lions Clubs had helped look after her here in the UK. We visited her at her father's farm and soon bottles of unlabeled red wine appeared along with bread and cheese and we were soon having a wonderful lunch. Her father spoke no English and it soon became apparent that we would not be leaving until we had drunk his stock of his very best wines, no matter how much we tried to hide our glasses. Our Lion President tried very hard to say no and eventually we all piled into the cars and headed back for a celebration dinner by which time our President was a very unpleasant shade of grey. After many toasts, he raised his glass and gracefully slid under the table, much to the merriment of our hosts. It was a very quiet drive back to the UK the next day with the cars laden with the wine and the cheese for a Beaujolais Nouveau party the following evening where the rest of the club could enjoy the benefits of our adventures.

In Scotton, we became involved in Dalmatian Rescue, which is covered in the Chapter on The Spotty Dog era, and now my focus is more on helping young people succeed in business and I am being trained as a Business Mentor with the Prince's Trust. I also served on the Parish Council in Scotton, which I found fascinating, but as my eyesight deteriorated I had to resign as the Chair as I was no longer able to read the plans and all the documentation involved.

I think it is critical that we put something back into our communities, as too often we get the impression that society owes us something, when I think it is us who society support.

Chapter 9: Travels and tribulations

I have always had wanderlust and loved to travel, from my earliest days in military service, through a spell in industry and then into my sales and marketing career, I have loved to meet people and explore new cultures. The first stop in any new venue was to a supermarket, to see how the natives shopped and what they ate. After that a restaurant to experience the cuisine of the area and always the rule of "when in Rome, eat like a Roman". A question I was often asked was which was my favourite destination. It's a very difficult one to answer, but India, Israel, and Italy always featured in my top three for a variety of reasons, perhaps more later.

But where to start? Perhaps in the village of Heinsen in the middle of a NATO exercise in April 1967, in an International Harvester M9A1 REME support Halftrack with a burnt-out clutch. These vehicles, our example of which was supposed to have come ashore on D-Day, had been converted to a mobile crane with a small shed on the back for the crew. This vehicle was designed to travel with armoured units and to lift the power-packs out of failed Armoured Fighting Vehicles (AFV's) so they could be repaired or replaced. Ours had a habit of burning out the clutch, and so I was left in charge of the vehicle, with a few slices of stale bread, a tin of Compo jam and a tin of Compo Irish stew, just in case. You'll recall the theory of Compo rations from Chapter 4. It was a great system when you could get a change of menu, but often, all you could get was one specific pack and no amount of whining and cajoling at the cookhouse brought any respite. When I say that everything was tinned, I mean everything. Here are the contents of Ration Pack Menu E (Late 1970)

Breakfast	Bacon and beans
Main meal	Soup
	Lancashire Hot Pot
	Fruit Dumpling and butterscotch sauce
Snack	Oatmeal Block
	Fruit biscuits
	Brown biscuits
	Cheese spread
	Chocolate bars (2 tins of 5), and boiled sweets

Travels and tribulations

The pack also contained:

Drinks   Chocolate drink
                    Beverage whitener
                    Sugar, tea and coffee
                    Veg stock drink
                    Orange or lemon powder

Sundries   Chewing gum
                    Weatherproof matches
                    Tissues
                    Water purifying tablets

So there I was stuck in a small village waiting for Recovery, which, when it arrived at 2 am in the morning, was in the form of a Leyland Heavy Recovery vehicle, the only vehicle that could not tow my halftrack, because the rear crane on the Leyland would foul the front lifting jig on the halftrack and wreck the vehicles. I was assured that there would be a low loader along in the morning to recover me back to Paderborn, and the Recovery crew were off to follow the battle. I awoke to a freezing cold morning, and set about trying to get some warmth into me. There was a small gasthaus across the road and the Irish Stew was soon warmed up, washed down with some coffee. At lunchtime, and with no sign of the low loader, there was a knock on the back door, and a young boy pointed to the Master Butchers across the road and indicated with his hands that I should come and eat. Clasping my trusty sub machine gun (SMG) I followed him into the kitchen to find a large German family and a huge table covered in all kinds of meat. The young daughter, who was learning English at school, told me to tuck in and I was soon enjoying a much-needed meal.

When you are on exercise and the battle is fluid, keeping clean can be the last thing on your mind, and the halftrack was not designed with creature comforts in mind. To tell the truth, I must have given off a ripe odour and the mother led me through to the bathroom and indicated that I should have a bath, so there I was when the door opened, Mutti appeared and took all my clothes leaving me with my trusty SMG and nothing else. An hour later and all was back and I could rejoin the family. No one turned up to recover me that day and by this time, the battle had moved beyond the range of my puny B47 radio set, and all the codes had changed anyway and I had no way of contacting anyone. But it was a good life, three cooked meals a day, vast quantities of Schnapps consumed in the attic shooting range with competitions between the British Army and the Master Butcher, and on the Thursday I was told that as the honoured guest I would be accorded the great honour of killing the pig. Now I have to tell you that I was a Telecommunications Technician, trained to fix radios and not to kill, but what can you do? So with a large hammer, a bolt device and much sadness the beast was despatched and was soon being butchered. I have to say that I didn't sleep well that night.

In the morning, there was a great commotion in the village. Someone at Paderborn had noticed that my SMG had not been returned to the Armoury and my bed had not been slept in, and it was suddenly realised that the half-track was missing and so they sent out a recce party and a low loader to try and find me. Everyone was invited into the kitchen. Plates of food appeared and toasts were drunk to my rescue and the prodigal son was returned home. On the way out of the village the convoy halted at the family's Schnell Imbis (fast food) stall and everyone was given a Bratwurst sausage, from the pig I had killed the previous day.

India was a much favored destination because of all the cultures and history, and no trip to India was complete without a journey by rail. Interestingly, there always seemed to be a disaster whilst I was in country. In December 1992 I was there when the Ayodh Mosque calamity occurred, and in September 1993 in the Oberoi Hotel Bangalore, I was woken about 4am in the morning to the sound of a freight train passing over some tracks nearby. I woke in the dark, and put on the light, and saw the concrete beam above my head rippling. Then I remembered, there are no rail tracks anywhere near Bangalore and the noise slowly dropped and the concrete beam stopped moving. I opened the door onto the verandah to be met by a clothed figure, who said in a light Aberdonian accent: "Well, that was interesting," and we both agreed to meet in the 24-hour café on the ground floor. As we sat sipping our tea, next to the floor to ceiling glass panels, we suddenly realised that we were in great danger should there be an aftershock from what had obviously been a major earthquake and quickly moved. Later that day I travelled home and it was not until I arrived at London Heathrow the next morning did I discover that there had been a major loss of life.

My agent, a wonderful character called Naag, even suggested that I should stop visiting as every time I did, something bad happened, and little did we know that I would be the next victim. In 1994 I was back in India and we had flown into Madras, now called Chennai, and on our way to the customer I saw the familiar sign of a British War Cemetery, with its white lettering on a khaki background. It is located in the town of Nandambakkam, near Chennai and is home to 856 Commonwealth burials. On our return from our customer visit, the driver pulled into the cemetery car park to let me have a few minutes to pay my respect the boys and to sign the Visitors Book. As I strode towards the entrance, my eyes fixed on the Sword of Remembrance, I completely missed the copper rods linking small concrete blocks to prevent anyone driving into the cemetery. They had been turned dark brown by the climate, and my left foot caught under the rod, I tipped forward and my right foot caught the rod and I literally flew into the cemetery, landing with a thud in a puddle. The driver had seen me go down, and rushed over, helped me to my feet, and started to dry me off and brush me down. My agent arrived, and said, with a mischievous grin: "If you want to join the boys here, it can be arranged." I regained control and insisted that I pay my respects even though my leg hurt badly, and after a while we were soon en route to the airport and flying to Bangalore. On arrival at the hotel, I went to my room, then went down to the Polo Club restaurant and had a meal, and on my return, got ready for bed. I took off my trousers and was shocked to see that me left leg was badly swollen and was black from the knee to my toes. I called reception and asked them to get the hotel doctor who soon appeared, checked me over and prescribed aspirin and vitamin C tablets. In the morning I was in real pain, and it was decided that I'd better go for an X-Ray at a local hospital. I was duly driven over there by a hotel car. On arrival I met the doctors and we chatted about the UK political scene and cricket, of which I know nothing, and then it was decided after much tea and biscuits that I should have the X-Ray. I was shown into a room and there in all its glory was an X-Ray machine that looked like Roentgen's second prototype, I was made comfortable, a pad was placed over a delicate area, a quick look at each other, a button was pushed, and everyone

Travels and tribulations

ran out the door slamming it behind them, and leaving me with a whirring, clunking, whining machine. All went quiet, the door opened and I was back in the surgery, where the news was that I had not broken anything, but had just suffered very serious bruising. Back in the hotel, I started to organise my casevac, back to the UK. I travelled out from Bangalore Airport, having been taken by the hotel taxi, and was handed over in a wheelchair, when some of the real adventure started. By that time, walking was a painful challenge and so I had to have a full body frisk in the wheelchair. This guy had probing fingers and as I wriggled and tried to accommodate his probings and pattings, it was to notice that my briefcase, containing the company laptop, was disappearing with a stranger beyond the X-Ray machine. Frantically gesticulating, I managed to attract the attention of a security guard and we were off in pursuit, but it was all a case of identical briefcases. Left at the bottom of the aircraft steps in the wheelchair, it was a beautiful evening and soon I was joined by the pilot who helped me up the stairs and into my seat. My seat companion that night saw I had issues and on hearing of my problems was keen to involve his consultant in Bombay (Mumbai). What a lovely caring people the Indians are, always keen to help, and to know all your problems. In Mumbai, it all fell apart. The agent tasked to move me from Domestic to International was nowhere to be seen and it was quite a walk to the Inter-Terminal bus stop. I got to the BA desk at the International Terminal to find out that my details had not been sent ahead, but after much negotiation I was allocated three seats to lay out on. After take-off, I managed to convince a delightful stewardess that I was in great pain and soon my leg was packed with chilled Champagne bottles and ice, alas not to drink, as I was in Economy. So ended a very interesting trip.

One of the most challenging trips was to Singapore, Taiwan and South Korea in my role as the Outsource Business Unit Manager for Parker Hannifin Seal Group, Chomerics Division, and accompanied by the US Global Outsource Business Unit Manager, Adam Shayevitz. Adam and I went way back and had co-operated on a number of projects, and he had lived in Taiwan and was proficient in Mandarin.

The Singapore section of the trip was uneventful, and we made our way to Taipei, which was a four and a half hour flight, which following business

Travels and tribulations

meetings and lunch meant that we arrived at around 1700. Willie Chen, who worked for our host company was there to meet us in a huge black Mercedes Benz, ran us out to the magnificent Grand Hotel Taipei. He dropped us off and said we would have dinner at 1900, and I stupidly expected a quiet dinner in the hotel, so turned up without tie or jacket to be told that we would be dining with the President of the company, Henry and some of his key staff in the same dining room used during the visit of the ex-Prime Minister Margaret Thatcher at the World Trade Centre, Taipei. Willy opened the boot of the car on our arrival and removed a case of six bottles of Chateau Margaux wines which we carried up to the exclusive dining room at the top of the World Trade Centre. Please remember that I was tired after a long journey, but my hosts were determined to introduce me to the ancient art of "gan bei". "Gan bei" in Mandarin, or "dry glass" is an unusual activity and seemed to centre on the President, Henry, taking pretend sips of the excellent Margaux wine, whilst I drank deeply of it, and as I approached the bottom of my glass, Henry would raise his glass and salute me with a Gan bei, which appeared to mean downing mine in one. The meal was outstanding, and with such an attentive host as Henry I was enjoying such luxuries as Abalone and fish stew.

After the meal, it was decided that we would go to Henry's favourite Karaoke bar and we headed off to downtown Taipei. Here I was introduced to a rather special venue, seated in comfort, whilst a "queen" paraded a series of young ladies to be our partners in karaoke. My biggest issue was that I had daughters of a similar age to these young ladies and the effects of the gan bei's and the journey took its toil and I fell asleep, a cardinal sin. I woke in the Mercedes en route to the hotel, and my next memory is of waking around 1200 the next day, naked in my bed, with an unlocked hotel room and no key!

It had been agreed that we would meet for lunch at noon and arrange the rest of our day. After some discussion we decided to visit a local Military cemetery so that we could pick up some history, then watch the famous Changing of the Guard at the Taipei Martyrs Shrine, a very impressive spectacle. It is said that they are so highly trained that they do not even blink during their period on guard, and that the light skin under the chinstrap is a badge of honour for these men. After that we headed up into the hills behind Taipei to visit the Yang Ming Mountains, after first calling at the hotel to pick up towels. As we walked

Travels and tribulations

from the car to the entrance of the Sun-Moon farm hot springs, Adam, my travelling companion, disappeared off to the bathroom, and Willy and I walked into a large circular area where queues of couples stood in line obviously waiting their turn. At the opposite end of this circular hall were two exits, one marked for females and one for men. "So what happens here then, Willy?", I asked, and he explained that the temperature in the baths was so high, that everyone, including parents, knew that the temperature was too high for any hanky panky to occur, so young couples would come here to check each other over before becoming too serious, Willy and his wife had come here for that very reason. I was fascinated and then we moved to the male entrance of the changing room, and my jaw dropped as I entered a room with a large circular tub with steam floating off the surface surrounded by naked men and boys, then it hit me, it would be naked bathing and I turned to Willy, to see him smiling. "Welcome to Rome, Mr. Terry," he said obviously referring to my "when in Rome" sessions when I had introduced him to English food. At that Adam re-appeared wearing swimming trunks. So it is the general rule that you wash each other's backs and soon Willy and I had bonded, both ignoring Adam! The water was very hot, around 50 degrees Celsius and difficult to get into and I was very conscious of all the fathers pointing to this strange white man and telling their sons they would grow up like me if they didn't eat their rice and noodles. It was a great experience, but Willy and Henry had one more treat in store before we went on to Seoul, South Korea.

On the Friday night I had disgraced myself by falling asleep in the karaoke bar after the gin bei session, and so it was that we had another fabulous banquet on the Monday night, but this time I was fully aware of gen bei and caught Henry a couple of times with a near full glass. This time we arrived at the Golden Age Club Karaoke bar with me in a reasonable state to be met by the queen, the lady who would oversee our evening and choose the girls who would sing with us. First Henry asked me to choose the Scotch Whisky we would be drinking, and I was presented with five bottles, all with labels I didn't recognise. One of the labels was marked Bond 9 Leith and I had worked in Mitchell Street in Leith in 1962 on leaving school and had memories of the whiskys stored there so chose that one and the heads nodded in agreement so I had made a good choice. Soon hands were clapped and we were joined by a group of young girls, all around the age of my daughters back home and I became very homesick as I had been travelling for nearly two weeks. My young lady was called YoYo and did not seem comfortable to be there, so the ever vigilant queen saw this and hands were clapped and YoYo departed to be replaced by Angel. It would appear that someone had sprayed a leopard skin print onto her body, and she came and sat beside me and we were soon talking like old friends. It became her turn to sing and she had the most wonderful voice, and as she turned to talk to one of her friends I tapped her on the shoulder to ask her to sing another song I recognised on the screen and at that moment I felt an electrical shock. I guessed she was holding a microphone with a poor earth connection, but her hands were empty, I touched her again and felt the shock a second time, she turned her head and smiled. "That is what life force feels like," she said with a smile. I turned to Willy, and asked him to take me back to the hotel, alone, shattered by the experience.

Spain was always a favourite destination, and I travelled there so often, always staying at the Hotel Orense 38, directly opposite the Madrid World Trade Centre where my distributor had their headquarters. I was so often here, and always first thing in the morning, that I would welcome the Managing Director, Xavier Fuentes to the office with freshly brewed coffee, and we often had a good discussion about the Spanish market as we waited for the staff to arrive. Spain was an excellent destination for a number of reasons, a great technical market so lots of challenges, lovely people and I made many friends here, but the worst bit was the long lunches (also known as siesta time) and the very late dinners. Sadly I am a pumpkin type of person and starting to eat after 10pm was a no-no for me, and I soon learned all the restaurants in Madrid that served food around 7pm much to the horror of my hosts. After many years of international travel, I had come up with a theory about "Day three" and one day in Madrid it sort of came to a head. I was standing talking to a young lady and we had become good friends, and her boss, seeing us standing so close, and knowing of previous issues with other people of my Company, decided that I was another no good English guy come to cause trouble, so he managed to squeeze between the young lady and myself, and back me off to protect her. "What are you talking to her about?" he demanded to know, and I started to explain the "Day three" theory. It is based on the premise that on day one of a business trip you are very focused, on day two, you are still focused, and on day three you become very homesick and miss your wife, and

Travels and tribulations

perhaps your eyes stray towards the ladies. On the fourth day you regain your focus, but on day five, things go from bad to worse and you become even more homesick, but usually you are going home so all is well. "And what is today?" he enquired, I put my arms around him, looked him in the eyes and said: "Day five my dear friend." His reaction was immediate and he shot out of my arms with his back firmly against the wall, daring me to come any closer. The young lady, who was in stitches of laughter, turned to me and said: "You are a bad man Mr. Terry with your wind ups!" and it took several minutes to explain the differences between wind as in weather and wind as to wind up a clock or person to much hilarity.

Chapter 10: Travels in Ireland

I first started to travel in Ireland after I joined the Intelligence Corps Territorial Army, and travelled across to Belfast, flying in Loganair De Havilland Twin Otters, very small twin-engined passenger planes flying out on a Friday night and back usually on the Sunday afternoon. During the weekend my job was to lecture and present on the current threat of SOXMIS teams for units that were travelling to BAOR for their summer camps and to train the Belfast part of the unit in skills military, and security. These flights were always cosy with a maximum of 18 passengers and sometimes you were lucky and had a stewardess on board. On one particular flight in a terrible snowstorm, and with the strobe lights flashing, giving the impression that the propellers had stopped and the snowflakes were stationary, all the lights in the cabin went out. For a few seconds panic reigned until the cockpit door slid open, and a voice from the gloom asked if we were all OK. Hearing nothing, the door slid shut, and the lights snapped back on, revealing a lot of white faces, and some very nervous glances.

Due to my day job, I would occasionally be dropped off at the airport, get a bus to the station and a train to Dublin, so that I could start as a salesman on the Monday morning, hiring a car and travelling round Eire, which could be fun. On one occasion, I was being driven to the airport in a Ford Escort estate, with the driver sitting beside me, with a Browning Hi-Power 9mm pistol clamped in his groin for our protection, as these were hazardous times. As the armed guards on the exit slid the gates open, the driver gunned the engine and we were off when we both noticed a white Transit van parked at the end of the road. As we approached, the back doors of the van flew open and we both expected a hail of bullets from an M60 machinegun to hit us, the driver had a particularly smelly accident, I thought my last moment had come, and a drunk fell out of the van and onto the road. It was a quiet but very odorous journey to the airport, and on my return to the Drill Hall in Edinburgh on the following Tuesday as the strain of what had happened and my continued working in Ireland, left me very nervous I resigned from the TA.

It is interesting when you wear two hats just how you react to incidents. On another occasion, I was walking through Belfast city centre and had stopped at some traffic lights when I got lost, no problem, I had a map in my inside jacket pocket, so I put my hand inside my jacket and caught a glimpse of movement out of the corner of my eye. I looked round and found myself staring down the barrel of an SLR rifle, with a pair of eyes staring straight at me. His head shook from side to side, warning me not to take my hand out of my jacket, the lights changed and the Landrover moved off, the barrel of the gun continuing to point straight at my head. He wasn't to know I was one of his, and that all I wanted was to look at a map, but I was always careful after that about putting my hands in my pockets.

We often had visitors to Ireland, and one time I had a newly-married American couple who were flying into Shannon Airport, where I would pick them up, then drive to some customers before we would visit the village where her ancestors had lived before emigrating to America. By now I was no longer in the Territorial Army, but I knew the dangers of "bandit country" and tried to convince them that it would be safer if we met the relatives somewhere away from the border, but all the arrangements had been made, so we arrived at Carrickmacross, and soon the party was in full fling with much hugging and kissing. It became obvious that I was not welcome at the party and so I went to sit in the car and read a book when I was approached by a number of young men. "You're a Brit soldier, aren't you" one said and I explained that I was merely a simple salesman doing a favour to some business colleagues. This did not impress them, so I was asked to open the boot, which was packed with luggage and samples and literature, and this was all duly searched. Unable to find anything incriminating they turned their attention to me just as the happy newlyweds turned up looking for me, and were quite annoyed that I was being dealt with in a very unfriendly manner. There was some discussion and we were soon on our way, towards Belfast and the safety of the North. As we passed through Dundalk and into Northern Ireland we could see the presence of the British Security Forces, and they realised what a dangerous position we had been in.

Not every trip to Ireland was so eventful, and the people in the main could be very charming, you just had to ensure that everything you did was well thought through and that any answers you gave did not cause offence, which could be so easily taken. On one business trip, I was to be joined at Dublin Airport by a colleague who was flying in from Heathrow. He was bringing with him a new demonstration box that consisted of flashing LED's and electronic counters that flashed up and down. He was the last one through the security barrier and I could see by his face that he was very angry, as he stormed across the concourse to me.

"Where have you been," I asked.

"Getting searched because they thought that your demo unit was a timer for a bomb, and I have been searched in places I didn't know existed."

I calmed him down, took him to the hotel and then we went into Dublin to my favourite restaurant called Reuters, long since gone. Reuters was famous for its waiting staff who all wore see through blouses and black cord trousers and black bow ties and little else, and I thought that this might calm him down. He had a very loud London accent, which he was very conscious of, and the night descended into farce, with him whispering and me struggling to hear. From there we drove across to Galway where we met Gardai en route who were unhappy that whilst both our names were on the paperwork, I was not driving, then onto the hotel where calling room service entailed phoning down to reception, then going down to tell them that their phone was ringing. After that we arrived at the Clare Hotel, near Limerick and now it started to descend into farce, as we were having problems getting information from our boss about our pay review that was overdue. We decided that we would celebrate anyway with a nice meal and a couple of beers, when a tall statuesque lady walked into the restaurant and my colleague stated that he was going to ask her to join us. I managed to convince him that this may not be a good idea, but on the way out we bumped into her again and she told us that we had left the lights on in our car and pointed to a very expensive Mercedes. I didn't have the heart to tell her we were driving a Ford Escort Estate, and at that my colleague insisted that we buy her a drink for her kindness and she promptly ordered a double Hennessy on the rocks, and that said goodbye to any pay increase we were likely to get.

The next night we ended up in Cork and were taken out to dinner and then to the Café Royal for a drink. My colleague sidled up to me, and whispered in my ear that he needed to go to the toilet, but he could see only men in the place and was becoming concerned. As he had a really nice Shirley Temple hairstyle I could begin to see his concerns as it dawned on us both that this was a gay venue, and as we both needed we ended up going together, much to the amusement of our host. The next day we flew home, him to Heathrow, and me to Edinburgh and I was never so happy to go home to peace and sanity. Travelling with my new salesman George soon taught me an awful lot of the way of the Irish. George was a Ballymena boy, and this was his first job in sales. Navigating was not his strong suit, and this was in the days before SatNav, and we were driving from Clonmel to Youghal which is a mainly dead North South route. Youghal was slightly west of the road junction, so in conversation I said:

"Not far now George, a right turn and we will stop for some lunch."

"No, it's a left turn," said George.

For a second I doubted myself, but remembered the advice of my old ATC CO Flt Lt John Syme, and said that I was sure that we would turn right. But George was adamant that we would turn left, and then I noticed that he had the road atlas such that the top indicated north, and to George, we would turn left, on the map, for Youghal.

"But George, we are heading South and Youghal is West, so we must turn right."

"And how do you know we are heading South?," he said with the confidence of a man who is always right.

"That would be the fact that we are driving into the sun, it's nearly 12 o'clock and we know that Youghal is West," I said, but George then came out and asked me what the reference to the sun was all about, and I vowed never to let him to navigate again.

With the onset of SatNav, I thought that my troubles with George would soon be over, but on one occasion we had entered the postcode into the SatNav and it had brought us to the wrong location. We were in a beautiful estate of bungalows and not in an Industrial Estate, so we called the office who checked the customer's web site which had a message on it not to use the postal address postcode, but to use the one on the web site. Now George had a SatNav built into the car and one I had bought him, and with no further ado entered the information into both. We turned round and the car said turn left and the other one said turn right! I asked George to pass me the one I had bought him, but he refused as my hand reached for the window control to throw it out of the car. We had many other adventures often ending up miles from the customer with George adamant that they had moved. I miss my travels with George.

Chapter 11: The Caravan adventures

So we decided we needed to have some way of relaxing away from the stresses and pressures at the weekend, and so I decided that we needed a caravan where we could all pack up and go and have jolly adventures in the woods. But how to convince Joan that this would be a good idea? Firstly I changed the company car from a Mitsubishi Galant boy racer saloon to a Renault Espace on the basis that we needed a "van" type vehicle to move exhibition equipment and such like. Next I had it fitted with a tow-bar, in case we needed to move a lot of exhibition equipment! Then I started to buy caravan magazines, which was the dead giveaway, and I was told in no uncertain terms that we would not be buying a caravan. Not to be put off, I then started to visit caravan showrooms to show Joan the luxuries of caravanning, and so it was that we started to look in the local papers for a cheap one. The only thing that Joan insisted was that it had to have an end bathroom. For those of you unfamiliar with caravan layouts, of which there are myriads, one third of the van would be the bathroom, one third the kitchen and one third the lounge/bedroom and into this would fit two large adults and two large Dalmatian dogs, Ben and Poppy. We found what we thought would be the perfect caravan in the shape of a Coachman VIP 460/2, but it turned out to be riddled with damp and cost a few bob to make roadworthy, and so it was that we headed for the Caravan Club site at Clumber Park on Valentine's Day, the 14th February for a trial run. It was a total disaster from the start. It was freezing and I couldn't get anything to work, no gas for the cooker and no heating and the only lights we could get were from the battery, so we set everything up and left to have a romantic dinner at a local Little Chef, and that too was a disaster, poor food, an interminable wait and a wife who was making very unromantic noises. We headed back to the caravan and snuggled into our sleeping bags, at least these were snug and warm, but, at 3am I woke needing the toilet, but I couldn't move, there was a heavy weight stopping me from getting my hands out and lowering the zip. "Joan" I called, "What?" came the response, "I can't move and I need the loo," I moaned. "Neither can I," she said, and we both realised that we each had 30kgs of Dalmatian snuggled up beside us and fast asleep. They had crept up alongside us as we slept and it took some wriggling and prodding to wake them up. Some friends joined us the next morning and we soon discovered that the main problem was in the wrong type of gas. We had some adventures

The caravan adventures

with the Coachman but decided we needed something more substantial and found a Hymer Nova 555 with two fixed full-size single beds, a large lounge area and a heavy sliding door to keep the dogs out at night! This was a beast of a caravan weighing in at 1.7 tonnes, and needed a big vehicle to tug it and so we upgraded to a 3-litre diesel Renault Grand Espace which fitted the bill perfectly. What a lot of car drivers don't realise is that with a 1.7 tonne vehicle and a 1.7 tonne caravan, you are actually the weight of a small truck and unless you keep the combination in tip-top condition then pulling out in front of a caravan, just because you think he is going to be slow and you want to be in front, can put you and anyone else in your car in great danger. On one occasion, travelling at or near the legal limit for a caravan on a long straight road I saw a car pull up at a junction not far ahead of me and just pull out to be in front. There was traffic coming the other way, so I had no option but to slam on the brakes, I flashed my lights, and two fingers were waved out of the driver's window. A mile ahead there were traffic lights that were turning red, and I was out of the car in a flash and asked the driver's female partner if she realised that the moron sitting behind the wheel had nearly been responsible for the death of her three children, who were sitting in the back with no seat belts on. Before he could respond I was back in the Espace, the lights had changed and as they had a row in the car, I pulled round them and drove off. "One day you are going to do something stupid like that and end up in A&E," said my ever patient wife, but the number of times people pulled out in front just because they don't want to follow a caravan can cause a heart attack to the caravan driver!

Our caravan seemed to be a rain magnet; we would load up in brilliant sunshine, with happy hearts and head towards our chosen site only to see clouds looming on the horizon as we got closer. As we had powered movers fitted to the new caravan, getting it on site was quite easy with a natty little remote control which allowed very precise maneuvering; the major challenge was putting up the awning in anything less than a breeze and bright blue skies. We soon had it down to a fine art, on site, stabilisers down, power and gas connected and switched on, kettle on, water connected, and toilet sorted, a cup of tea and then extract the awning. By this time you could see the other caravaners settling down with their mugs of tea to watch the ensuing drama as you fought tooth and nail to get the awning up in a small gale that had

The caravan adventures

sprung up from nowhere. Our Hymer Nova was a big tall caravan and by the time I had the awning erected, I was exhausted and spent the next two days recovering before dismantling it and packing away a very wet, heavy awning for drying out before the next adventure. There were good times too, and it was very relaxing once everything was in place – but getting back could be stressful. On one occasion, the rig didn't feel quite right and people coming the other way kept flashing us, so eventually we stopped to investigate and could find nothing wrong. We called out recovery and they tugged us the few miles to home where we found out that the company that had replaced the two front tyres recently hadn't properly tightened the bolts and the two front wheels were about to come off! A few choice words were spoken and a very valuable lesson learned. On another time on the M25 just where four lanes became three the catalytic convertor failed, warning lights sprang on all over the instrument panel and the engine went into very low power mode and we got off the motorway just in time. The dogs seemed to enjoy travelling on the back of a low loader, looking down on the world, but this was supposed to be a stress-relieving hobby. The dogs really enjoyed caravanning because it usually meant a good walk through the woods around the site and they could often be seen at the window eyeing up the rabbits as they enjoyed the grass. It was interesting to see how some people could be so stupid with their dogs. Ours were always on a lead and always controlled with treats and biscuits, they would wander by and say: "He'll be alright, he just wants to play" but our dogs were part of a pack, and we all had roles to fill, I was the Alpha, or Boss dog, Joan was the dominant bitch, Poppy thought she was, and Ben's job was to protect the pack. Any approaching dog therefore was seen as an issue. He would start barking to alert the pack, and Poppy would join in, thus, bedlam. But he just wants to play, and he is off the lead and not under control, and it was always our dogs that got the blame, just for being part of the pack.

Sad old Sadie joined the pack having been thrown out of a car in Hull just for being old. When we first met her she was in a dreadful state, so we decided she might like caravanning. The first thing we had to do was buy a three-step entry for her as she had problems getting in and out, and she loved just lying in the sun watching the world go by. Quite often, we would arrange a bed and breakfast for Joan's dad Jack, and he would join us in the mornings and enjoy the sun with Sadie by his side. Seeing him home in the evening could be quite

The caravan adventures

humorous as we walked down the road each with a dog, Joan with Ben, me with Poppy and Jack with Sadie, difficult to tell sometimes where the grumbling and the passing of wind was coming from. "It's the damned dog," he would say, too quickly perhaps.

Caravanning drew to a close as I started to have problems with my eyes and Joan declined to learn how to tow. So we decided that the beast had to go, but we wanted it to go to a good home, we put it on a site on the Internet and watched and waited as virtually no-one showed any interest in it. Eventually we had a couple of questions from an interested party and we sent them detailed pictures of what they wanted to see. Eventually they came to view and I had set up the whole thing, except awning, on our drive and left them to look over it. The clincher was that we would go with them to their first caravan site and set it up with them, and then go back in the morning to help them take it down, as we knew they were the right people for our beloved beast. For some months after, we received e-mails and pictures from all over as they ate their fish and chips in some interesting locations.

It took some time to sell the Espace too, but it also went to a good home and shortly after that I had to stop driving for a while until I had major eye surgery on my right eye, but the caravan days were over.

Chapter 12: The Spotty Dogs

We got involved with Dalmatians by accident really. We had been cat people, starting with Scraggs that adopted Joan at Bradford University and turned out to have a belly full of kittens, an issue that was soon resolved. After our wedding in April 1973 and our move into Married Quarters in Old Dalby, Scraggs soon developed a taste for quiet country life and became a victim to a tractor whilst sleeping in the middle of the road. A visit to Leicester and we became the proud owners of Trouble and Strife (the wife) and they travelled with us between Old Dalby, Bradford and Edinburgh. In fact Trouble, a rather sleek black cat with a small white bow tie decided to consummate the marriage on the parcel shelf of our Hillman Avenger southbound on the A68, and as the noises of animal passion rose from the rear of the car I noticed that the car behind was becoming dangerously close as the occupants became focused on the events before them. I pulled into a layby only to have them follow us in, but by this time Trouble had completed the mission and they drove off. We moved to Rosyth with three cats and on losing the last one, Trouble, to old age, found two new kittens, Murky and Mindy, Murky being a sleek black cat with a white bow tie, the apparent re-incarnation of Trouble. He too lived to a good age, until one night he had a stroke and we became catless again. By now we were living in Scotton in Lincolnshire, in a very quiet village surrounded by woodland walks, and it seemed that a dog would be a better choice and would give us much-needed exercise. A visit to a local dog rescue centre, and Little Ben joined the family, said to be a much-loved pet of a family who claimed in a letter given to us by the rescue centre that he was a perfect pet in every way. He was said to be a Border Collie cross, but in reality turned out to be a cross Border Collie, in fact a psycho dog who appeared to hate everything that moved, especially policemen!

We only had Little Ben for a short while but in that time he taught us an awful lot about dealing with an aggressive unhappy dog and that is where the title of the book comes from, as I had to become Boss Dog and sort him out. We were expelled from dog training classes after he started a fight between two Bronze Standard Alsatians, and caused havoc at the other class we attended briefly. One day whilst I was travelling to Gatwick, to fly to the US on business, Joan was walking him down a quiet lane and he was checking out the hedgerow

The spotty dogs

for rabbits, the school bus trundled round the corner and quick as a flash he attacked with inevitable consequences. He was killed outright but it wasn't until I arrived at the hotel late that night that Joan was able to tell me what had happened, and I feel so sorry for the people in the adjacent rooms as I howled out in grief at the loss of my dog. In the morning, the strangest thing happened as I sat in the plane waiting to depart for Boston, I sensed that Little Ben was beside me, I stroked him gently, and he was off, perhaps to wait for me at the Rainbow Bridge.

On my return it was obvious that we would need another dog, and a chance find of a book on Dalmatians in a sale and the breed was chosen. We approached the British Dalmatian Welfare Service but were told in no uncertain terms that we were unsuitable to adopt a Dalmatian! No interview, no home check, just no, despite us fulfilling all the necessary requirements, so we started looking at puppies, and Joan was very unhappy at the thought of a seven-week-old mite joining our pack. Her persistence paid off and we were off to visit Caroline, who had a Dalmatian rejected by a family with young children, something we were soon to find out was the result of 101 and 102 Dalmatian films being shown on the television. We arrived at the farm house to be met by four Dalmatians bounding up to us, led by Brian. Two bitch Dalmatians and a puppy bitch Dalmatian following in his wake and what a fabulous dog he looked, in tip top condition.

Caroline joined us and after a thorough grilling about our intentions, and having walked him in the fields, Brian, now renamed Ben, was in the back of our car, en route to Newark to acquire all the necessaries for a large dog. We knew we had made the right decision, when on returning to the car we found not total destruction, but him fast asleep on the back seat. We visited Caroline on several more occasions, one to see Ben's mums new pups, little toothpaste tubes of pure white with legs, and on each occasion, the little bitch puppy tried to bond with me, playing with my shoe laces and running round my legs. Called Poppy, or Top Totie at Tumbril, she had been bred to compete for Best of Breed at Crufts 2003, but had turned out to be deaf in her right ear, and so could not be bred from, and was now just an extra mouth. We had always planned to have two dogs and it was soon agreed that we would fund her spaying, and she would join Ben, or Tumbril Travelling Man, at Scotton.

The spotty dogs

We joined all three mainland Dalmatian clubs and were soon involved in helping out the Welfare Services of each club, moving Dalmatians around the country and spending weekends at either dog shows, or parked up at Motorway Service areas waiting for a dog, or new owner to turn up. We soon realised that the Mitsubishi Galant saloon had to go and the Company soon acquired a Renault Espace people mover that acquired a large two-bay crate for transferring dogs. It became apparent that there were issues with the North of England Dalmatian Club (NoEDC) Welfare Service, and I set up a meeting with the Chairman with Joan's comment ringing in my ears: "Do not bring the Dog phone home." The meeting with the Chairman was amicable, and I was soon homeward bound with two boxes of loose folders and bits of paper and the dreaded Dog phone. If I had known how much it would have transformed our lives, I would never have touched it, but there was obviously a need for order and structure and soon with the help of friends and colleagues in the NoEDC we had an understanding of how many dogs were adopted out, and a means of logging and qualifying dogs and homes so that we could start taking the messages off the phone.

You learn very quickly in such a situation, and we soon learned to dread those awful words: "I love him to bits – but..." that we were to hear from so many people. It was the 'but' and you had to quickly ascertain just what the 'but' was.

"...but he has just eaten the kitchen"

"...but he has just eaten next door's whole chicken. Raw"

"...but he has just stolen an ice-cream out of my baby's mouth"

Or worst of all: "...but he has just bitten my partner," which was a virtual death sentence as it would be impossible to re-home a known biter. The risks would be too great.

One of the saddest 'buts' was the "...but we are having to downsize, and the old dog has to go." Never the young dog, who could be sold, but the old dog that no-one would want. The intention was that we would have the heartache of euthanising the dog, and it would be on our conscience and not theirs.

We also got a number of dogs and bitches from dog rescues and shelters, and they were some of the saddest. Often they would come and live with our pack until nature took its toll, or until they could be moved on. Each one is a story

The spotty dogs

in its own right, but ones that deserve a mention include sad old Sadie, Whispa, and Trenton. My eldest daughter was married at Rudstone Walk, South Cave in April 2008, and while I was returning people to their various homes on the Monday I got a call from Joan to say we had to go back to South Cave. When I asked what we had left behind, she told me that there was an eight-year-old Dalmatian bitch stray being put to sleep on the Friday as her seven days would have expired then. It was agreed that we would visit the next day, which I had already booked as a holiday to recover from the wedding, and so we set off. On arrival at the Rescue Centre Joan went to do the paperwork and I went to interview the Dallie, and met the saddest, smelliest, most dejected Dalmatian I had ever seen. She had been bundled out of a car at the side of the road, and left to fend for herself. The worst thing was she would not look at me at all, any attempt to look into her eyes and she would shuffle away. She had lost all her trust and faith in humans, and had given up. I checked her over, she had a missing claw, had so many lumps and bumps that I guessed they had got rid of her either because they couldn't be bothered to put her to sleep themselves, or thought there was a big Vet bill looming, and she wasn't eight years old, she was thirteen if she was a day.

I took her back to the Rescue office with tears streaming down my face and Joan and I agreed that we would take responsibility for her and would pick her up on the Saturday, taking her straight to the Vet for a checkover. The Vet spent some time fussing over and turned to us and said: "Well, there is good news and bad news." "So what is the good news?," I asked? "If she lasts the weekend, it will be a miracle." And the bad news? "All the lumps and bumps seem benign, and her heart seems sound, she has just had the stuffing knocked out of her. What will you do with her?," she enquired. There was only one solution, she would have to fit into the pack at home, and see if we couldn't convince her that some humans could be trusted. We introduced her to Ben and Poppy; she walked into the house, chose the best bed, looked at the other two and went to sleep for a day. Over the next nine months she had a whale of a time, we took her caravanning, having bought a special three-level Granny step to get her in and out, and she especially loved a slow leisurely walk round Laughton Forest, but her walks became shorter and shorter until one day I came home from work to find Joan cuddling her on the floor as she waited for the Vet. She was seen off in style, and her ashes are now scattered around her favorite walk.

The spotty dogs

Whispa was probably the most beautiful liver-spotted Dalmatian I had ever seen; I met him at a Rescue Kennels and went into his cage to interview him. It was soon obvious that he was stone deaf, a common problem with Dalmatians, but he looked great and I would have loved to have seen his pedigree. He had been found wandering and the Dog Warden had picked him up. Towards the end of the interview, he put his paws on my shoulders, his muzzle under my chin, and hugged me. With a lump in my throat, I knew I couldn't put him to sleep, which was the only practical solution, and he too joined our pack as we learnt to live with a deaf Dalmatian. We tried everything to find him a new home to no avail, and eventually stumbled across Lizzies Barn in South Wales, and they agreed to take Whispa if I delivered him to the barn. I chose a Bank Holiday weekend with a Cup Final in Cardiff to make the trip and just after lunch delivered him to the Barn. What an amazing place, three separate packs living in close proximity and the dogs deciding which pack was best for them. Whispa was introduced to his pack one dog at a time and the first one was a Great Dane bitch who licked him from end to end, knocking him off his feet. Lizzie had told me that she liked every dog to have a purpose and that Whispa was to be the eyes of a blind Siberian Husky! At that the door opened and in walked the Husky, across the yard and straight into Whispa, who sniffed his muzzle, licked his ears and the two wandered off across the yard, just touching as Whispa led him away. I turned to Lizzie with tears streaming down my face, unable to talk, hugged her and left to complete an epic 11 hour round trip. Lizzie taught Whispa to respond to hand signals and to a blue torch, something that dogs can see clearly, and he was soon adopted out to live on the South Coast but sadly there was no happy ending as I later found out that someone had laid out poisoned bait and he died.

Trenton was the last old boy to share our house, thrown into the Trent to get rid of him, he managed to stay afloat until he was rescued and handed over to the Dog Warden, who handed him to the Rescue Centre we knew so well. When we met him he could barely stand, they had to feed him by placing his bowl between his paws so he could dip his head in and pick at the food to build his strength. He came home in the car, wandered into the house, picked a quiet corner and slumped down, the look telling Ben and Poppy that he was not a threat and this would be his spot. Over the weeks he built up his strength but his walks were limited to less than 200 yards, before he would turn for home and sleep. Mealtimes were a hoot because that was when he came alive; barking so loudly that his front paws would leave the ground and grinding his teeth. Sadly time soon got the better of him, the Vet thought he was probably about 15 years old, and he too was covered with lumps and bumps and so it was that the Vet came. I tried to sit in the same room, but his deep dark eyes bored into mine and I knew that he understood. I left the room and the deed was done and I was able to go back in and bid him farewell. He was a stunning dog, so obedient and so gentle and affectionate, I miss him so much.

One day we got a call from a colleague asking us to rescue a Dalmatian that was in grave danger, so we drove to a house where we met a beautiful boy called Casper who apparently had been attacked by a neighbor's dog. I walked out of the house to check him over and he seemed fine, definitely not nervous, or frightened and we were soon off to his new home, where he would be living with an elderly bitch Dalmatian. A few grumbles when they first met, and we were on our way knowing that there was another happy ending, but we could not have been further from the truth. After a few months I took a call from South Yorkshire Constabulary asking whether or not I knew of the location of Casper, as he was deemed a dangerous dog and was to be put to sleep for killing another dog and biting its owner. My first reaction was that I knew of no such dog, but alarm bells rang and I was soon on my way to Casper's house to warn his adopters about the risk and to check him out. On my arrival, I was given a cup of tea, and Casper cuddled up to me on the sofa nuzzling my ear with delight at seeing me again. This wasn't a dangerous dog, something was wrong.

I was approached by a lawyer and asked whether or not I would be an Expert Witness for Casper in an upcoming hearing. I readily agreed, as this was not a dangerous dog, all my instincts told me so and soon I had completed a three page Expert Witness statement, dealing with how big dogs warn off little dogs as they have no real defence against them as little dogs can run between their legs and come up at the throat, the most vulnerable part of a dog. I gave my evidence, and noted that the head of the Bench kept nodding as I gave my opinion, obviously someone who understood big dogs. I turned out that the little dog had died from crush injuries and not bite wounds, caused when the owner had fallen on it whilst trying to hit Casper with his stick, so I had been right all along. On my way home, I called in at Casper's home to deliver the

The spotty dogs

good news only to have my ears nuzzled again. What a nice dog.

We gave up running the NoEDC Welfare in 2010, handing it over to a willing volunteer and for the first time in ten years were able to come home and not dread looking at the home and Dog phones. It had dominated our lives for ten years, I had had to learn to cook as the first thing Joan would do when getting in from work would be to get the messages of the phones and e-mails and start calling out. If I wanted to eat, then it was down to me and my skills started to improve, as, with five sisters, a ten-year Army career and marrying a superb cook, there hadn't been a need before.

All we have left now is Poppy. She sleeps all the time and snores terribly, and I am told that there will be no more dogs when she goes, but I bet there is an old Spotty dog out there that will need our love and care.

I have mentioned the Rainbow Bridge a couple of times, and you either believe in it or not, but I leave you with this story:

The Rainbow Bridge

It was a quiet time at the Bridge and several old dogs were lying quietly, waiting for their owners to arrive and take them over the Bridge and through the gates into a better place. Time stood still here, there was no illness or pain, and occasionally a dog would sit up, ears twitching, and an old figure would walk up the hill towards the Bridge, the dog would run over, a quick sniff and then the fussing of the ears and the pair would walk over the Bridge and into the light. Suddenly there was pandemonium; an old lady was walking up the hill, and all sorts of dogs and cats rushed down the hill and started to fuss around her. Puppies and kittens, old dogs skipping like youngsters, her steps quickened and her back straightened as she reached the Bridge. "What's going on, said one dog waiting for his owner, they can't all belong to her, can they?" "No" said the other dog. "She is a Rescue person and can take through all the dogs and cats that were not loved." And as she passed over, they all went with her.

Chapter 13: Cruising and schmoozing

Having lost the ability to drive due to problems with my eyesight, and not enjoying long-haul flight as much as I used to, we looked around for another way to enjoy vacations and we stumbled across the Norwegian Cruise Line site and saw they had a new ship coming into service called the Norwegian Gem. She would be sailing from Dover to Barcelona on her inaugural voyage. I discovered that this massive ship was being built in the middle of Germany at a place called Papenburg, and was soon enjoying the views of her being constructed in a big shed. On completion she would be sailed down the Ems Canal to Rotterdam, where she would complete her acceptance trials before her first ever cruise. We also discovered the Cruise Critic website and soon had most of our questions answered before we even set foot on her. Her inaugural cruise departed Dover on the 8th October 2007, and she visited Vigo in Spain, Lisbon, Portugal, Gibraltar, Naples, Civitavecchia and Livorno in Italy and Nice, France before heading to Barcelona where she would operate from before departing to the USA. We chose mini-Suite 11538 portside mid-ships on deck 11, so as to reduce the effects of motion, but we need not have bothered as she was so well built and equipped we never really noticed any motion. She was a magnificent vessel, and I was soon exploring all the venues and features available to us in our mini-Suite. You get no real perks in a mini-Suite except for a large cabin, but what we had was excellent and we were very happy on board. As we were members of the Cruise Critic Roll Call, on the first sea day there is a meeting called the "Meet and Greet" in the Le Bistro restaurant, where you get to meet the Captain and the officers and your fellow Cruise Critic members, and it was a pleasure to see so many attend. I had been following Captain Mikael Hilden's activities as he had sailed the Gem through the very narrow passages on the Ems Canal and as the meeting broke up and the officers mingled, our eyes met and he came over and I was able to get some time with him discussing the challenges. Every so often, one of his officers would pass by, "Everything OK Captain?" and he would wave them away as we continued to discuss the challenges he had met. Eventually he moved off, but we had been marked by a number of his team as someone the Captain found interesting!

As we departed Lisbon some days later on the deck watching everything we

Cruising and schmoozing

became involved in conversation with Claudio, the Concierge. He had been at the Meet and Greet, and I addressed him as the famous Claudio, as he featured on the Cruise Critic NCL forum. He asked us if we were enjoying the cruise and we said we were, but I explained that we were lowly 'mini-Suite' passengers – but he had been one of the people checking up on the Captain. We chatted for a while and he invited us to have breakfast the next morning in his Restaurant which was exclusively for Suite guests, and he was gone. The nest morning we turned up at the allotted hour, and started to introduce ourselves to be met with "Oh, welcome Mr. and Mrs. Terry" and we were whisked into the inner sanctum and had one of the best breakfasts ever. Was it a cunning plan for us to book a future cruise in a Suite? If it was it certainly worked, and we have done so ever since.

Given that there are 2,400 odd passengers and 1,500 odd crew aboard, it is interesting how you keep bumping into the same people time and again. On the Gem, we decided one day to eat at the Great Outdoors café at the back of the ship under a large awning and there were only two seats left at a table. I asked if we might join them and was taken aback by his comment that he was a US Air Force Baptist padre, but we were welcome to join them. That's okay I said I am a Scottish Agnostic, and the four of us soon became good friends, bumping into each other again and again and having dinner on three occasions. Such is the pleasure of cruising.

Our next cruise saw us departing Scunthorpe by train to Barcelona which was the start of a 24-hour adventure via Doncaster, London Kings Cross, London St Pancras, Paris Gare du Nord, Paris Gare d'Austerlitz and on to Barcelona on the overnight sleeper, the Joan Miro which arrives in Barcelona at 0943 in perfect time to be at the front of the queue at the Cruise Terminal. We had booked a Romance Suite, 10666, at the stern and thus were able to quickly reach the front of the queue and were soon getting our keys from Ruth the Concierge before being shown to our Suite to meet our Butler, who introduced-herself as Mother Theresa. From the sparkle in her eyes I have to confess she did not look like a Saint so became known to us both as Momma "T", a name she seemed delighted with and later on another cruise, we noticed her at the Captain's Cocktail party, and the look of sheer delight as she noticed us was very special. The cruise took us out into the Atlantic and our first port of call

Cruising and schmoozing

was Casablanca, which was our first time in Morocco, The Grand Mosque was an amazing sight and the sheer size tended to overwhelm you. Back on board and we had an uneventful trip until on the way back towards Gibraltar, we endured quite a storm but the view from the stern over our balcony had to be seen to be believed. Back in Barcelona, we stayed in a local hotel for a couple of nights before heading back to the railway station for another 24-hour adventure on the trains, certainly a great way to travel.

Now completely bitten by the cruising bug, we booked a two week back-to-back cruise out of Venice this time at the very front of the ship directly under the bridge in Suite 10500, which would give us spectacular views of Venice and beyond and we were certainly not disappointed. The view from just under the bridge was magnificent and the walk from the Suite to breakfast or lunch certainly brought some much needed exercise. On this cruise we met many of the officers and had a very enjoyable time, preferring to have a quiet time on board chatting to the staff. On one trip ashore at Izmir, we had a great adventure; we saw the museum and the historical attractions and were then dropped off at the Clock Square where we would have some time in the bazaar before meeting the coach again near the Clock Square at 2 pm. We strolled off into the bazaar where we were soon approached by a short Turkish gentleman, with near perfect English, who wanted to sell us a shirt or two. He accurately guessed my size, and led us off to his 'uncle's' shop who stocked these sizes. As we got deeper and deeper into the bazaar, we both became a little nervous but we were soon at the shop and we chose two shirts that seemed a reasonable bargain. Our friend had promised to show us the way back to the Clock Square, but now he had our money and he waved his arm in a general direction as he sped off to snare another poor unsuspecting victim. Now, as a road warrior of some repute, I knew we had to keep turning left to get back, but my wife Joan was insistent that we turned right. Added to that we heard the sounds of music and drums banging and it was obvious that there was some form of event taking place. When you are in a bazaar, with narrow streets and high walls you find out that your so called Smartphone isn't so smart as it cannot see enough satellites to get a fix and so we started to keep turning left, and after a few minutes we met the first of a number of groups of riot police, all helmeted and with shields and batons drawn. "Smile," I called to Joan, "then they know you are not a threat." We carried on for some distance, still turning left and asked some people if they spoke English to no avail, and the clock ticked inexorably towards 2 o'clock. We turned back briefly as we saw the anti-Government demonstration wending its way towards us before noticing a group of motorcycle policemen standing on a junction, so I approached one who was a giant of a man. Before I could utter a word, he reached out his hand and shook mine and said: "Welcome to my country, how can I help you?" and I explained that we were under a tight deadline and needed to find the Clock Square. "It's only 200 metres, keep turning left" he said, before asking us where we were from. I explained that we were from Scotland, and he grabbed my hand again and said: "Jimmy" before laughing and sending us on our way. Just 200 metres on, we turned left and there was the coach with five minutes to spare. I must confess to being very hot and bothered once I got on the coach, but soon recovered my usual good humour.

We decided to celebrate our 40th wedding anniversary and my retirement on board our favourite ship, the Norwegian Jade, and whilst we had originally booked the same cabin, as luck would have it, we managed to get an upgrade to the Black Diamond Suite, the only suite on Deck 15 and it was fabulous, our own little romantic suite on the top of the ship. On arrival at the ship in Civitavecchia near Rome we found out that not only was Carlos Zarate with whom we had become good friends still the Concierge, but that there were several others of the crew who remembered us from the previous voyage and the fun began all over again. Wherever we went, we were met with smiles and hugs and it was quite a wonderful experience.

So where left to cruise to? This all started with a desire to cruise to Alaska, but we are planning to cruise to Canada from New York, and possibly through the Panama Canal from Los Angeles to Miami with friends we met from Australia. Who knows; time will tell.

Chapter 14: In search of Business Excellence

So what exactly is Business Excellence, and why is it so important? You can have an excellent business, you can have a business that is performing well in the current climate, you can have a business that has an excellent management team and you can have a business that has an excellent supply chain, but, have they all achieved Business Excellence?

I suppose I have striven for Business Excellence all my commercial life, and have been helped on that journey by some amazing mentors, teachers and role models. I have learnt different skills and abilities from each one, and always made sure that any successes I had from their advice and guidance was fed back to them. My first Sales Manager was a wily old bird called Ron Adams for whom I worked for four years in MCP Electronics, a company based in Wembley. He told me to go and learn my products, learn my patch, and start to learn my selling skills and when he thought I was ready he would send me on an advanced selling course to polish off the edges and it worked perfectly. On the way I met some amazing people, the best sales person I ever met was Larry Tucker, VP of International Sales at Thermalloy, Dallas, Texas and a day spent with Larry was worth a month in a classroom, knowledgeable, intuitive, polite and hugely knowledgeable about the products and their application, I used him as a role model to this day, though he is sadly no longer with us. Sometimes it is good to be exposed to the other side of the coin, and time spent with the man who was always late, showed me it is better to always be five minutes early, giving time to gather your thoughts and composure and to use the facilities. Americans could be a challenge and Bill Jordan, President of Thermalloy had a way of testing whether or not you knew your customer well, by always asking where the bathroom was. I knew about this and on arrival at a major defence contractor, asked Charlie the Security guard if he wanted a coffee and got it for him exactly as he liked it. Bill was impressed and never asked for the bathroom again, showing that knowledge is power.

Other guides and mentors include Georges Patounas, an expert in body language, and I learned a huge amount from him whether in the classroom or in the field. His book Silent Language is a classic, and well worth reading if you can find a copy. One of his observations is with regard to the "square

In search of business excellence

metre" that surrounds us all. Some people are comfortable with you entering their bubble, but many are not, and apparently according to Georges this includes your glass if you are in a bar. Put your glass too close to someone else's and if they move theirs, they find you intrusive and if they don't but put theirs closer to yours after taking a drink, shows they find you not unattractive.

On the mentoring front I have been blessed with knowing some great people such as Colin Guthrie of Kingsway Consulting and Peter Brent of Mathieson Brent Consulting. Both have been great in their wise and sage advice which I intend to use in my future with the Prince's Trust as a Business Mentor. Watching, listening and learning is all part of aspiring to Business Excellence, but two of the most important ingredients are passion for your company and people, and a vision as to what looks good and what the future holds. I call it my 'I see' skill, seeing what looks good in the future, and knowing how to get there from the now. A lot of people scoff at this, but I find that time spent at the beginning of a project, identifying the background of the venture, the experiences of those involved and the "unique selling points" of the products that are to be sold or marketed is invaluable, and then by looking into the future to what would look good with the product or service can show a route to success. Sometimes, due to many circumstances, the client's vision or route can be seen to lead to disaster and it can take the patience of a saint to gently inform the client of the potential for a train wreck of an outcome.

Over the years I have encountered many different solutions that are intended to take you to Business Excellence, many coming from the Asia/Pacific but all seemingly designed to cut costs to the bone, thus giving the impression that Business Excellence is all about profit. I have been told that you have to be lean, holding little or no stock, and with the minimum of staff, so when there is an upturn in business you struggle to meet the demands of the market. That, and minimum order values placed on you by your suppliers, can be a real pain, as they want you to hold the stock they don't want to hold, thereby leaving you in a vulnerable position if the market slumps.

At HITEK Electronic Materials Ltd a company located in Scunthorpe, I was head hunted in by the owners from one of their major suppliers to run the company on the retirement of the second owner, the first having retired some time before. The company had been formed fifteen years previously when Emerson and Cuming, part of the W. R. Grace empire, closed its factory in the town and moved all its European manufacturing to Belgium. It was a very interesting operation, with a very diverse range of people, with two married couples and relatives all working in what was essentially a two bedroom house with a large shed on the back. It was quite complicated with hot desking going on in one office and no privacy whatsoever, so if I wanted a quiet chat with someone or to discuss some failure then the local garden centre was where you ended up. Everyone knew that an invite to the garden centre could be career limiting, so most people avoided an invitation to lunch.

The company had been struggling with sales for a couple of years, and with' some 'big' company ideas, it was soon turned round and I saw twelve years of continuous growth before handing the reins over to my number two, and retiring into the sunset. Towards the end of my tenure we entered a competition to win an award for Innovation and at the Northern Lincolnshire Business Awards ceremony. We not only won the Kimberly Clark Award for Innovation, but also the Forrestor Boyd award for Business Excellence, a fitting end to my career. Since leaving HITEK they have gone on the win the NDI Award for Business Excellence, and I had the privilege to attending the event where the award was promptly dedicated to me, a real honour.

So what is the true meaning of Business Excellence? It is all about Premier Customer Satisfaction, where a customer keeps coming back because he knows you care about him and his issues. HITEK was set up to run the ethos of yes, if a customer phoned up wanting product the next day, provided you had stock and available labour, then the answer was always yes, and sometimes I would get a call from a customer saying:
"Yesterday you promised me fifty gaskets today."
"Have they arrived?," I would ask, only to be told that they had arrived and could he have another fifty tomorrow, and the answer of course was yes. On one occasion a major customer, who had a habit of phoning up and telling us we were rubbish for a one day late delivery, was put through to me by one of the Sales team. "He is complaining about a late delivery," she said, "but we have nothing on the system." I took the call, and it was soon obvious that he had blundered and had not ordered a critical part. We had material in stock,

because I didn't believe in lean, so I explained that we were not late as he had not ordered the part. The phone was slammed down, and ten minutes later he was back on the phone complaining that we were late and yes there was the order on the fax machine with a delivery date of the next day. Our carrier had already left, and so it was that I was on the first train out of Scunthorpe station clutching the part for delivery by hand before twelve noon. So was he happy, no, he didn't turn up for work that day due to an incident the previous evening, but I made sure his boss knew that he had received Premier Customer Service.

Chapter 15: Would you follow this man into battle?

Firstly, as I told you at the beginning, of the book, a speech, presentation or book has to have a beginning, a middle and an ending, and as I start to bring this adventure to a close I have to admit that I have never been in combat, so why the title of this last chapter? From the age of thirteen I have been involved in one way or another with the military, and one of the things I learnt was how to quickly assess the likelihood of the success of following someone into battle. There are three likely outcomes:

• Yes, you would follow this man into battle, he has leader and survival written all over him, and usually it is a handshake and a look into that person's eyes that tells you all you need to know.

• No, he will get you killed, but it might be interesting to see how he meets his inevitable fate.

• You cannot follow someone into battle that is hiding behind you and pushing you forward. If you survive then they immediately step into the limelight to claim the credit.

It was a few years ago that I was heading for a meeting with a colleague when I suddenly stopped in my tracks. A thought had popped into my mind, and it formed what another friend and business acquaintance might call a 'tipping point'. I turned to my colleague and asked him if he remembered my comments about my thoughts on judging people on the "follow into battle" theory. He agreed that he knew my philosophy, so I asked him if he would follow me into battle, as I had suddenly realised that I was not the one following into battle any more, but had become the one leading. He thought carefully before looking me straight in the eyes and then offered me his hand, "Yes, I would follow you into battle," he said and we went into the meeting in a much stronger position and won the business.

As I came to the end of my current business career I knew that I would need a challenge to keep me not only occupied, but out from under the feet of my long-suffering wife Joan. I suspected that my old company HITEK might need access to my skills and abilities, so I decided to form a small consultancy to advise SME's (Small to Medium Enterprises) to do business with the Ministry of Defence and the major Defence contractors. Given the hair colour, I soon came up with the name Argent Vulpes Ltd and so the company was born, with just two staff, but a mountain of information and intelligence available within. But why Argent Vulpes, I hear you say? Easy. Argent is the tincture of silver,

Would you follow this man into battle?

and belongs to the class of light tinctures, called "metals" and Vulpes is the genus of the Canidae family. Its members are referred to as 'true foxes' So after fifty years after leaving school because I could not handle Latin, I end up forming a company with a Latin name.

So from having served The Queen, worked in industry, travelled the world, been a Boss dog, had a wonderful marriage with two beautiful daughters, what is left, you ask. I was sitting on Doncaster station platform en route to Leeds when I was approached by someone conducting a survey, name, age, occupation, reason for journey, came the questions, then she stopped to ask me why a 65-year-old retired person was going to Leeds for an interview, and I explained about the Prince's Trust and my desire to help young people succeed in business. She wished me well.

I only hope that in 65 years' time, both Charlotte and Jack, our Grandchildren can look back on such exciting lives as I have had. *Slàinte mhath*

.